Mission-Based Alignment

Take Your Company to the Top
and Keep It There

Mission-Based Alignment

Take Your Company to the Top and Keep It There

Robert K. Bennett
William R. Lingar

ATLANTIC
PUBLISHERS & DISTRIBUTORS (P) LTD

Published by

ATLANTIC

PUBLISHERS & DISTRIBUTORS (P) LTD

B-2, Vishal Enclave, Opp. Rajouri Garden,
New Delhi-110027
Phones : 25413460, 25429987, 25466842

Sales Office
7/22, Ansari Road, Darya Ganj,
New Delhi-110002
Phones : 23273880, 23275880, 23280451
Fax : 91-11-23285873
web : www.atlanticbooks.com
e-mail : info@atlanticbooks.com

ISBN 978-81-269-0843-1

Printed in India
at Syndicate Binders, Noida-201305

Contents

Introduction

IBM Chairman Sam Palmisano calls sustainable competitive advantage "the holy grail of strategic thinking". He says that the central question for every CEO is, "how do you come up with a business model that differentiates you and that creates value for your customers, and, by doing that, puts you in a unique position in your industry?"

Several years ago, we began searching for answers to several vexing questions:

- Why do some companies stay on top of their industry while others seem to falter?
- Why do some founders score extraordinary successes with their start-ups and then seem to be unable to repeat the performance with a new start-up?
- Why do some companies achieve stardom at the top of their industry and then inexplicably start to fumble and decline?
- Why do top rate consulting companies score wins on some clients but seem to have no impact on others?

In our search we discovered that the companies who remained at the top of their game shared seven principles. Most of these companies were still led by their founder. When the founder departed the scene, those who succeeded the founder often departed from some of those principles and consequently performance declined.

Once we were able to recognize and delineate these seven principles, we asked ourselves, how can we teach and help companies to institutionalize? How can we turn an art into a science? This led to the creation and development of Mission-Based Alignment (MBA)—a business planning and management system that will help companies develop an innovative and unique business model that is focused on the customer need. If faithfully followed, MBA will lead to a sustainable competitive advantage.

Part I

Understanding the MBA Mindset

Seven Guiding Principles

1

Do you remember TWA and Pan Am? Twenty years ago, they were both large, international airlines. Today, they are, for all practical purposes, gone.

Digital Equipment Company (DEC) was once the dominant manufacturer of mini-computers. It is gone. (So are mini-computers.)

Radio Corporation of America (RCA) was a very large manufacturer of consumer electronics. It is gone. Its name may remain, but the company is gone.

You may not remember the real Western Union. In the early 20th century, it was one of the largest and most powerful companies in the U.S. The Western Union you see now is not that company. Another company bought the rights to use the name. Western Union, the company, is gone.

AT&T, the American Telephone & Telegraph Company—Ma Bell—has been swallowed up into one of her children, SBC (Southwestern Bell).

What do all of these companies have in common?

- They lost contact with their customers.
- They failed to understand the shifting needs of their customers.
- They failed to define the future for their customers.

Other companies, sometimes after redefining themselves, continue to perform at the top of their game.

By 1993, IBM's annual net losses reached a record $8 billion. Cost management and streamlining became a chief concern. And IBM considered splitting its divisions into separate independent businesses.

Louis V. Gerstner, Jr. arrived as IBM's chairman and CEO on April 1, 1993. Soon after he arrived, he had to take dramatic action to stabilize the company. These steps included rebuilding IBM's product line, continuing to shrink the workforce and making significant cost reductions. Despite mounting pressure to split IBM into separate, independent companies, Gerstner decided to keep the company together. Gerstner redefined IBM's mission and aligned the company to that mission. Today, IBM is thriving.

Steve Jobs was one of the founders of Apple Computer. In the early 1980's, at the urging of the Board of Directors (who thought the company needed "adult leadership"), Jobs brought John Sculley, a well-known management veteran, into Apple as CEO. As the Macintosh took off in sales and became a big hit, John Sculley felt Jobs was hurting the company and persuaded the board to strip him of all power. John Sculley tried to change the discipline of the company by controlling costs, reducing overhead, and rationalizing product lines. Jobs left Apple and started a new computer company called NeXT. He also bought Pixar for $10 million. Meanwhile, Sculley was dismissed, and the Apple Board hired Gil Amelio as Apple CEO with the mission to enhance shareholder value. (As we will discuss later, if your primary purpose and mission is to enhance shareholder value, you won't succeed.) Predictably, Amelio failed. After Gil Amelio's departure, Apple purchased NeXT Computer, probably to bring Jobs back into Apple. Jobs returned to Apple as interim CEO. Subsequently, the word "interim" was removed from his title, and he has re-energized the company.

In 1965, Yale University undergraduate Frederick W. Smith wrote a term paper about the passenger route systems used by most airfreight shippers, which he viewed as economically inadequate. Smith wrote of the need for shippers to have a system designed specifically for airfreight that could accommodate time-sensitive shipments such as medicines, computer parts and electronics.

Federal Express was incorporated in June of 1971 and officially began operations on April 17, 1973, with the launch of 14 small aircraft from Memphis International Airport. On that night, Federal Express delivered 186 packages to 25 U.S. cities from Rochester, NY, to Miami, Fla. Though the company did not show a profit until July 1975, it soon became the premier carrier of high-priority goods in the marketplace and the standard setter for the industry it established. FedEx has a customer-focused mission. It remains a powerhouse in overnight delivery and is still led by CEO Fred Smith.

Why do some companies soar and others languish? Why do winners who have dominated their markets and industry for some time—companies such as Sears, Toys R Us, and General Motors—suddenly stumble?

Consistently dominant winners have obviously achieved a sustainable competitive advantage. But how did they do it? And what is it about them that gives them their sustainable competitive advantage?

For years, we have been searching for the secret and have finally uncovered Seven Guiding Principles, which are followed by all companies who have consistently remained at the top of their industries. Furthermore, we have learned that if other companies adopt and adhere to these Seven Principles, they, too, are likely to experience sudden, dramatic, and sustainable improvement in their results and will overtake and pass other companies on their way to the top. The Seven Principles lead to sustainable competitive advantage by producing a unique, customer centric business model that cannot be duplicated, because it incorporates the psyche of the company's leader.

THE SEVEN GUIDING PRINCIPLES OF TOP PERFORMING COMPANIES

1. Successful companies keep their central focus and top priority on the customer and his/her need.
2. Successful companies identify and select their customers.
3. Successful companies differentiate how they serve the recognized need of the selected and identified customer in ways that provide real, recognizable value to the customer.
4. Successful companies develop and promulgate prioritized values that truly reflect the business values

of the leadership and tell the employees how the company will operate on a day-to-day basis.

5. All of the decisions, initiatives, directions, investments, plans, procedures, policies, actions, and reactions of the company are brought into alignment with the central focus and the mission.
6. The leadership preaches the mission throughout the company with a religious-like zeal and commitment. All employees buy into the mission. And the buy-in takes place from the top down—in that order.
7. Every employee, including the CEO, subordinates his or her needs to the needs of the company.

Before we discuss the Seven Guiding Principles in more depth, a couple of cautionary notes:

- This is not sloganeering. It is not sufficient to write the Principles down, frame them, and hang them on the wall in the reception area, down the hall, or in the employees' break room. Successful companies fervently believe in these Guiding Principles and follow them in everything they do, 100% of the time. To do less is, at best, a waste of time and, more often, actually harmful.
- At first glance, following these Principles may seem simple and easy. Knowing what to do may be easy. Consistently doing it 100% of the time is not so easy.
- Some people have maintained that these Principles and the underlying business theory are naïve and overly simplistic. We take the opposite view. We believe that too many business leaders and managers over complicate business to their detriment and the detriment of the business. As we will discuss at great length later, everyone in a business—**every employee**—must know, understand, accept, and ultimately embrace

  - who the company is,
  - what the company plans to become,
  - who the company's customer is,

- what that customer needs, and
- how the company will serve that need.

In our model, these and other concepts are embodied in the Mission. In order to achieve as wide an understanding and acceptance as possible of the Mission, leadership and management should strive to simplify its Principles and underlying business theory as much as possible, reducing miscommunication, misunderstanding, and confusion to a minimum.

Let's review and discuss each Principle.

1. Successful companies keep their central focus and top priority on the customer and his/her need

Every company has three main constituencies—customers, employees, and owners. Sure, there are other constituencies, such as suppliers and the community within which the company resides and operates, but most agree that the primary constituencies are customers, employees and owners.

A fundamental key to becoming and remaining a top performer is the priority a company and its leaders place on these constituencies. They must be addressed in the order we have named them—customers first, employees second, and owners third.

A company's leader often must juggle many balls at the same time. However, there is usually one area of concern that primarily occupies the leader's mind—that subject that he or she thinks about when he or she goes to bed at night and gets up in the morning; that area where he or she has the greatest sense of urgency. In our studies, we have found that this area is usually one of the following four:

- Solving each day's problems;
- Beating the competition;
- Profits (enhancing owner or shareholder value); or
- Meeting the customer need.

Some leaders and managers spend their days reacting to and solving the problems that come across their desks. They go home at night feeling they have done a good job if their desks are clear at the end of the day. Not only are these leaders and managers not taking their companies anywhere, they are failing to recognize and understand that too much "fire fighting" is a symptom of a company that is in bad shape—a company that does not have its elements in alignment and is not focused on its Mission.

Many leaders and managers are focused—even obsessed—with beating the competition. We agree that knowing what your competitors are doing is important, because they may have detected a change in a customer need that you haven't yet recognized. However, if your primary focus is on the competition, then you aren't focusing on the customer, and you will never be first—never in the lead. You will forever be reacting to someone else's moves.

Other leaders and managers focus on profits or enhancing shareholder value. In fact, most business schools still teach profits as the primary purpose of business. The CEOs of companies that are highly and consistently successful know (or have learned) that profit is a measure of performance—not the purpose or central focus of the company. If you send a message throughout the company that profit is the number one concern, then employees will make decisions and set priorities every day that are keyed and focused on maximizing profit rather than serving the customer. As we will discuss later, financial strength is important and, therefore, making a healthy profit is also important. However, it cannot and must not be the primary focus.

The only proper primary focus is the customer and his/her need. It is the only focus that can propel the company into a top performing position. All companies who are consistently top performers place the customer first in their list of constituencies.

2. Successful companies identify and select their customers

Some companies try to be all things to all people. Successful companies know that by focusing in on a selected customer segment, they can better understand and serve the needs of that customer, building a strong relationship and loyalty with the customer. Companies who serve the needs of their customer most closely will capture the hearts and minds of those customers.

In turn, the customers develop a certain loyalty to that company and continue to do business with that company for reasons that go beyond price.

Companies who try to be all things to all people are trying to serve such diverse needs that they never develop a capability and reputation for serving any particular need particularly well. Therefore, because there is no other outstanding reason for a customer to decide to buy that company's products or services, price becomes the driving factor in the customer's decision to choose that company or another company. All top performers have developed reasons other than merely price for their customers to continue to return to them for their needs that are served by that company.

3. Successful companies differentiate how they serve the recognized need of the selected and identified customer in ways that provide real, recognizable value to the customer

Differentiation is an important key to sustainable success. If a company understands that its primary focus is to serve the customer need and it clearly selects the customer that it chooses to serve, then it can develop ways to serve that customer's need that are clearly different from the other competitors who also try to serve that need. Moreover, successful companies differentiate themselves in ways that have clear and obvious value to that customer.

Dell Computer selected the business computer user and differentiated itself by selling directly to their customers with computers assembled to order and delivered quickly. Dell's computers are certainly not the cheapest. Nevertheless, Dell understood and met the needs of its selected customers and continues to win out over its competitors.

After Steve Jobs was invited out of Apple, the company drifted, trying to enhance shareholder value. Jobs returned and brought back a fierce focus on the selected customer. Whereas those who led the company during the time he was gone tried to make Apple more like Compaq Computer, Jobs re-instituted a distinct differentiation. The results speak for themselves.

Highly successful companies differentiate themselves and maintain that difference. Unsuccessful companies do not differentiate.

4. Successful companies develop and promulgate prioritized values that truly reflect the business values of the leadership and tell the employees how the company will operate on a day-to-day basis

Leaders of successful companies know that the success of the company depends on the performance of its employees. Therefore, it is imperative that each and every employee understands the company's priorities, how the company wants them to conduct their day-to-day business, and what values the company holds as important. By developing, prioritizing, and disseminating its values, the company is giving its employees a simple, handy guide for their day-to-day actions. Without such guidance, employees will make it up as they go along or superimpose their own values.

5. All of the decisions, initiatives, directions, investments, plans, procedures, policies, actions, and reactions of the company are brought into alignment with the central focus and the Mission

It is useless for the leaders and top managers to develop a clear understanding and plan for where they want to take the company if the rest of the employees don't know about it or have barriers and obstacles placed in their paths which hinder them from following the plan and achieving its goals. Most unsuccessful companies who think they have a plan have day-to-day procedures, policies, decisions, initiatives, incentives, directives, budgets, and investments that motivate and lead people to make decisions, take actions, and produce results that are not in line with the plan.

Leaders of successful companies ensure that every communication with the employee—every written document, every directive from a manager or supervisor, every training course, every incentive plan, every list of departmental and personal objectives, every behavior which is rewarded or discouraged—is consistent with the company's goals, objectives, plans and strategies. Everywhere the employee turns; everything he/she reads or hears; every decision he/she sees made by management; that employee sees consistency with the plan.

6. The leadership preaches the Mission throughout the company with a religious-like zeal and commitment. All employees buy into the Mission. And the buy-in takes place from the top down—in that order

Too often, we have seen top executives hold an all-too-infrequent meeting with employees and talk about financial measures, such as margins, profits, and inventory turns. This is a major mistake for several reasons:

- Employees don't understand and don't care about such matters, because they generally don't understand the financial dynamics of the business and, to the extent that they do understand, they don't believe that, individually, they can affect these results (and they are right).
- It turns the employees "off" to the prospect of employee meetings.
- It squanders a valuable chance to talk about the customer, that customer's need, and the Mission—things the employee can relate to.

Leaders of successful companies have a deep sense of who the company is, where it is going, and how it is going to get there. They constantly communicate this message to the troops at every opportunity. Leaders of successful companies are forever talking about the customer and his/her need. They preach this to everyone in the company at every opportunity as if it is a religious conviction.

7. Every employee, including the CEO, subordinates his or her needs to the needs of the company

High employee morale is important to a company's success. The morale at Apple, which was in the dumpster before Jobs returned, has soared. However, while the needs of the employees are important and are not ignored by successful companies, the needs of the business take precedence. The needs of the business must come first. Then and only then will the primary need of the employee—to be a part of a stable organization that controls its own destiny—be met.

MISSION-BASED ALIGNMENT (MBA)

After we understood that successful companies have these Seven Guiding Principles in common, we asked ourselves what business management system we could develop that would help client companies consistently follow and adhere to these Seven Guiding Principles on a daily basis. In answering that question, we developed a powerful, new management system called Mission-Based Alignment (MBA), which, when installed and followed, provides a simple road map for adhering to the Seven Principles, thereby improving performance and exhibiting a new, high level of business excellence.

In a way, Mission-Based Alignment is not new nor does it depart from recent advances and thinking in management theory and practice. Rather it combines various advances in the art of management into a holistic view that transforms the art into a science, which can be studied, learned, and utilized by anyone.

In recent years, a significant amount of money and time have been spent by companies on consultants such as Accenture to upgrade corporate technology within the corporate environment. Too many of these efforts met with mixed results. Too often, the same consultants succeeded at one client, delivering much if not all of what was expected, only to fall significantly short at the next client.

Did the consultants somehow go dumb—forgetting what they knew and how they did it? We don't think so. Mission-Based Alignment shows us that the technology they were upgrading at companies where their results were poor was, in all probability, not the right technology. As a result, no amount of upgrading and streamlining would change the wrong (unaligned) technology into the right (aligned) technology.

Other consultants have concentrated on process re-engineering, many times with similar results—spotty and unpredictable. Again, Mission-Based Alignment reveals that no amount of re-engineering will turn wrong (unaligned) processes into correct (aligned) processes.

When the technology or the processes are out of alignment, they first must be brought back into alignment before they can be re-engineered, refined or upgraded. Otherwise, the company is not only throwing its money away, it is wasting valuable time and frustrating its employees by creating expectations of improvements that don't materialize.

Marketing experts have exhorted us to "delight the customer" with no clear explanation as to why this is important. In fact, many executives went through the following mental process:

> "If I please the customer more than my competitor does, my costs will be higher than my competitor's costs. Yet if I can't charge more, my profits will be less. Therefore, what I should do is attempt to match my competitor in customer satisfaction."

We have heard this (or words to that effect) often. However, Mission-Based Alignment teaches us that you can and should charge the customer more if you delight him or her, and the customer will be happy to pay it!

The biggest tragedy has occurred in lay-offs, a practice that is so common and visible that it has fostered a whole new set of euphemisms—downsizing, "right" sizing, reorganizing. In England, employees who are laid off are referred to as "being made redundant".

During the Harold Geneen years at ITT, conducting a lay-off (this was prior to coining the phrase "downsizing") was a rite of passage from lower management into middle management. It was the way an ITT manager "made his bones". Never mind that, within three months, most of the employees who had been laid off were rehired or replaced with other employees at the same or higher pay rates. The lay-offs were widely heralded within the ranks of ITT's upper management, while the rehires went unnoticed.

Wall Street analysts and, in particular, fund managers love downsizing and will reward management with a bump up in the stock price. If a downsizing is done as part of bringing the company into alignment, it is still tragic but is nevertheless necessary to save the remainder of the company. If, however, it is done to appease analysts and fund managers or because the CEO doesn't want to be the only one in his golf foursome who hasn't downsized, it has devastating effects on the company (including on those employees who remain employed at the company—the "survivors") with no offsetting benefits whatever.

Why do some companies succeed and others decline?

GE	AT&T
CostCo	Sears
FedEx	General Motors
GEICO	Toys R Us

We also looked at companies that have succeeded and companies that have declined and asked, "Why"? For example, the companies shown above on the left are continually successful and among the tops in their industries, whereas the companies on the right were once at the top but then declined. Are the executives at successful companies smarter? Did the others suddenly get dumb, or did the Board of Directors replace smart executives with dumb executives? We think not.

We all know of companies, such as Toys R Us, where the founding executive left and the company's performance declined. Was the founding executive a better or smarter manager? Again, we think not. We think there is another explanation. Necessity is not only the mother of invention; it can also be the mother of strategy. Founding executives are often focused on the customer because they have no choice. This customer focus became ingrained, and the founding executive continued this customer focus because that's who brought him to the dance. Intense focus on the customer need is a central tenet of Mission-Based Alignment.

Sometimes, when the founding executive finally departs the scene, the replacement CEO is not as focused on the customer. When this happens, the company begins to drift into non-alignment, and performance declines.

Mission-Based Alignment pulls all of these efforts, such as

process re-engineering, technology improvements, technology upgrades, initiatives to "delight" the customer, and even downsizing, together into a whole. With Mission-Based Alignment, we understand the importance of these various initiatives. We also understand how and why they must all be in balance-aligned, if you will. If these and other elements are not aligned, each of these efforts, taken alone, will cost more and produce less (in some cases, a lot less) than originally hoped or promised.

In this book, we examine many companies' results, including some of the companies listed earlier. None of the companies we will discuss have been our clients. Our comments and analyses are based on public information and our observations are "from the outside looking in".

All companies have problems. As we will discuss later, perfect alignment is an unattainable goal. Companies are constantly either moving towards or away from alignment. Therefore, there are always opportunities for improvement.

Also, most of a company's problems are usually not apparent to outside observers. When a company does appear to an outsider to have troubles, it is usually a safe bet that their problems are deeper and more severe than we can see. So, in most cases, the "troubled" companies we will discuss in this book are "more troubled" than we describe.

How can a business leader know if his or her businesses are out of alignment? There are several symptoms that are relatively easy to detect and which always indicate an alignment problem.

LOW MARGINS

Companies who are not aligned have lower margins than their best competitors—in particular, lower gross margins. Gross margin (or gross profit, if you prefer) is the margin that remains after direct costs are subtracted from net sales. Direct costs are those costs that in the short-term rise and fall with sales; i.e. costs that are directly variable to sales volume.

For example, if a manufacturer's sales rise, the manufacturer hires more assembly line workers and purchases more parts (raw material, assemblies, components, etc.) that are needed to make the products. Conversely, if sales decline, fewer parts are ordered, and fewer workers are needed.

Gross margin dollars are available to cover indirect costs (sales and marketing, R&D, and G&A expenses). After we subtract these indirect expenses, we have operating margin, which becomes available to pay bank interest, taxes, and profit.

Within a narrow range, most companies pay the same in a given geographic region for workers. Also, within a narrow range, most companies should pay about the same for their material (assuming comparable quality). If these costs were all similar, then why would one company have a significantly higher gross margin percentage than another? There are two common reasons.

One variable might be price. There is a natural price range within which customers will pay for a product or service. If a company attempts to charge a price that is higher than the top of the natural price range, the customer will find an alternative for the product or service or do without, because the value of the product or service to the customer is less than the price asked. If the natural price range for the product or service is too low for a company to make a profit, then the product or service will be offered by the gray or black market (flea markets, etc.).

The company with the higher gross margin charges more for its product or service; e.g. at the high end of the natural price range. And why can they do this? Because the customer is willing to pay more. And why is the customer willing to pay more? Because the value perceived by the customer, based on the total experience of doing business with that company, is high enough to warrant that price!

The other driver of higher margins is that aligned companies have less waste. Mission-Based Alignment exposes wasteful investments and expenditures that are eliminated as part of the natural alignment process.

If gross margins are higher, then all other margins, including profit, can be higher. **Alignment is more important to margins than any other single factor, including size.**

FIGHTING FIRES

As we will discuss later under Systems, the work performed in a business has three "system" elements: people, processes and tools (technology). The tools can be as simple as a hammer or as complex as a computer. The processes are the flow of tasks and activities.

- The quality of the process determines the effectiveness of the system;
- The quality of the technology determines the efficiency of the system; and
- The quality of the people determines the responsiveness of the system.

In an aligned company, systems are geared to satisfying a customer's need in an effective, efficient and responsive manner. Responsiveness is measured first by the ability to detect and recognize the subtle, ongoing changes in the customer's need; and secondly by the ability to act quickly and proactively on those changes.

In the misaligned company, responsiveness means fighting crisis fires. When fire fighting becomes the accepted norm, it sets the standard for how we measure managers, which tends to be based on their crisis management skills. While the short-term perspective of crisis management appears to be responsive, productive and justifiable, from the long-term perspective crisis management is none of these things. In actuality, fire fighting results from the need to "react" and "recover" from an organizational mis-alignment between the needs and wants of the customer and what the organization is actually delivering to that customer.

Many common symptoms of organizational misalignment, such as internal conflicts, customer complaints, and high employee turnover, are viewed or rationalized by some managers as events which lie outside the control of management. Therefore, the ability to fight crisis fires becomes a standard and desired quality of successful managers. As a result, the short-term goals of success, such as increasing revenues and cutting costs, receive the bulk of management's attention; and the direct connection between their daily crisis fires and the decay of business processes goes completely undetected.

Most managers do understand that responsiveness is very important, to the point that they have elevated responsiveness to the highest priority in the system—above effectiveness and above efficiency—and that, too, is a problem. An organizational crisis is a result of an ineffective process—a misalignment between what the customer wants and needs and what the organization delivers. The harder we work to respond to the crisis, the faster the process decays. As a process decays, the system needs more and more responsive energy to function. Then, we fill the short-term gap of a broken process with more people, because in the short-term perspective, people are cheaper.

We end up with more people and less process. The imbalance continues to feed on itself in a downward spiral. Due to burnout and turnover, we are finally forced to change the people in the equation. Any remaining processes that exist begin to evolve around the skills and experience of the new people filling the short-term gap. With the loss of the more experienced people, additional people are needed the help fill a new gap. At some point, the "responsive people cost" is so high that we are finally able to justify the cost of bringing in additional technology.

So, instead of finding the proper balance of effectiveness, efficiency and responsiveness in our system, we end up with bureaucracy. Lots of technology, lots of people, weak processes, and customers who remain dissatisfied.

Most organizations tend to respond directly or indirectly to crises as a team. When they do, they stray from the mission as a team. The leader is also a follower, following signs and trends and carefully reading trends as "indicators", which can be internal as well as external. If there is a slight trend to drift away from the mission, perhaps in response to a crisis, and the trend continues without correction, the business faces the danger of "mission creep". In other words, *crisis management becomes the mission*. The leadership must be disciplined enough to bring the organization back to the proper Mission. **The most important role of the leadership of an organization is to keep the organization focused on the Mission.**

The next important role is establishing balance and alignment. Symptoms such as low morale and crisis management are signs many leadership teams fail to notice. Unfortunately, they are signs of misalignment and imbalance. Both management and leadership require skills of balance. For managers, it is balancing organizational systems. For leaders, it is balancing discipline and innovation.

Organizations that perform with excellence know the needs of their customers and have missions, strategies, structures and systems which meet those needs and exceed expectations. These organizations are aligned with the needs of their customers and in tune with themselves. Because they consistently fulfill the needs of their customers, crises and the necessity to respond to them are rare.

Internal Conflicts

An atmosphere of labor/management conflict indicates an alignment problem. Conflict among managers is also a misalignment indicator. Conflicts occur when there is disagreement on what should be done, how it should be done, or in what order things should be done. When there is no agreement on these issues, there is no direction. If there is no direction, there is no Mission. If there is no Mission, there can be no progress.

Customer Complaints

An aligned organization has relatively few customer complaints. One core ingredient of alignment is intense focus on the customer and his/her need. In aligned companies, an increasing trend in customer complaints is a key danger signal that the company is becoming less aligned and must take immediate action to reverse the trend.

Different Agendas

Whether the agendas are hidden or out in the open, if different executives and/or managers are marching to different drummers, the company is, by definition, out of alignment, because there is no commonly embraced Mission. If there is no commonly embraced Mission, there is no Mission, irrespective of what the leadership might believe and profess. Different agendas are also a central cause of conflict among managers.

Employee Morale

Morale is directly proportional to alignment. The better the alignment—the higher the morale. The opposite is also true.

As they do with customer complaints, aligned companies track employee morale. If morale is improving, the company is moving towards alignment. If morale is deteriorating, the company is becoming less aligned, and it must detect and correct the causes.

Internal Focus

Companies that focus internally rather than on the customer need are by definition out of alignment. The most common internal focus is cost control or cost cutting. However, if you have no Mission and no Strategy, how on earth can you know which costs you can cut and which costs are necessary?

"They" versus "We"

A company's relative alignment can be gauged by a simple test. Have an outsider engage an employee in conversation. If the employee refers to the company as "they" rather than "we", the company is out of alignment. Moreover, the higher in the company the employee is who says "they", the more misaligned the company is.

Mission-Based Alignment begins and ends with the customer. Sandwiched between the customer's need and the customer's reward for choosing the company for his/her product or service needs are all of the focus, planning, actions and fulfillment engaged in by the company to serve the customer need. We refer to these elements—focus, planning, actions and fulfillment—as Directives, since they form a progression of activities and decisions throughout the planning and execution process that direct the company and its employees toward serving the customer need.

The next chapter will explain the Seven Guiding Principles and the corresponding MBA Directives—one-by-one. Then, we will put them all together and discuss how and why Mission-

Based Alignment is the one and only winning planning and management system for businesses that want to succeed and prosper.

MBA Directives

2

PRINCIPLE #1: THE PURPOSE OF A COMPANY IS TO SERVE A RECOGNIZED CUSTOMER NEED

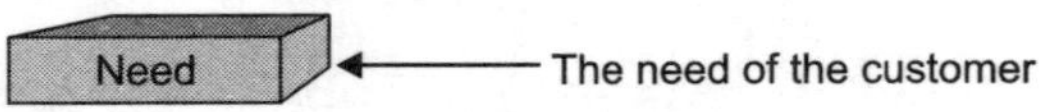

The Need must be recognized, not created

VisiCalc

Computer Output Microfilm

Apple's Newton

Dow Jones Online Market Report

Mission-Based Alignment begins and ends with the customer and his/her need. This customer need cannot be created in the mind of the company or its executives—it must be recognized and understood. Fans of the TV show Kung Fu will say that the company's leaders must become "one" with the customer. The leaders must understand the customer need as fully and deeply as possible. If they can achieve this level of understanding, then they will "know" where that need is heading and will recognize and respond to changes in the need as soon as they are detected.

Above, we listed four examples of understood and misunderstood need. We'll briefly discuss each one in order to illustrate what we mean by recognizing, as opposed to creating, a need.

VisiCalc, written by a team of programmers under the direction of a man named Dan Bricklin, was the first spreadsheet program. VisiCalc fulfilled at least two needs in the marketplace.

- A spreadsheet was a godsend for managers who had to develop budgets, sales projections, etc. VisiCalc allowed them to do "what if" exercises without the need for a box of number 2 pencils and a lot of erasers. You could change one number and instantly see the effect of that change on the bottom line without manually recalculating all the numbers. Prior to spreadsheets, developing a budget or a business model was a time consuming and error-ridden process.

- VisiCalc also provided justification for those people (primarily engineers) who wanted their company to purchase a microcomputer for them. At last, there was now an honest-to-god, business-oriented program they could run on the machine, which gave them the justification they needed for the purchase.

Parenthetically, VisiCalc also produced two other effects. It just so happens that it was written for the Apple computer. (This was before IBM had entered the PC business. There were no clones, no standard MS DOS operating system, and no standard Intel chip.) Apple was merely one of many manufacturers of microcomputers. Today, all of the other microcomputer manufacturers of that time except Apple are gone, and while Steve Jobs deserves a lot of credit for what he has done, and continues to do, with the company, he should thank Dan Bricklin for writing VisiCalc for the Apple.

The other effect was that a young programmer on Dan Bricklin's VisiCalc team named Mitch Kapor later started a company called Lotus and developed Lotus 1-2-3, the first user-friendly spreadsheet program.

Therefore, although VisiCalc was a first of its kind, a new spreadsheet program when there were no such animals around before it, it was not a pursuit of a new technology for the sake of technology. It clearly fulfilled a need among customers—a need that Dan Bricklin recognized—and was very successful.

Computer Output Microfilm (COM) was not so fortunate. In the early '70's, computer memory was still rather costly. Large users needed a method to archive old computer records and files without creating a mountain of paper (or so Kodak thought), and self-proclaimed visionaries were predicting that the "paperless" office was just around the corner.

So, a new technology—COM, which allowed the computer to write directly to microfilm—was developed. The industry—especially Kodak—loved COM. The trade magazines loved COM. The customers didn't need COM. While COM was being developed, the cost of memory began dropping like a rock. In the end, users merely added more memory to keep files active for a longer period of time, archived what they needed to keep on paper, and deleted the rest. COM was a dismal failure.

In the late '80's and early '90's, many within the PC industry thought that the handheld computer was the next big product. Apple spent a lot of R&D energy and dollars on the Newton—Apple's first Personal Digital Assistant (PDA). The product bombed and began a deterioration at Apple that continued until Steve Jobs returned to become Interim CEO. Some blamed the handwriting recognition software, which was not up to snuff. Others blamed the lack of applications. The reasons don't matter. Newton and its other handheld computer brethren did not fill any recognized need.

Dow Jones, the publisher of *The Wall Street Journal*, has been searching for two decades for new ways—primarily ways based on electronics and/or telecommunications—to package and sell the vast amount of financial news it gathers everyday. During the mid-'80's they developed a service whereby they would broadcast over their own nationwide radio network news flashes about various companies. Subscribers would pre-designate which companies they were interested in hearing about. Based on the subscriber's input, Dow Jones would program and deliver to them a small box. Then, prior to each new announcement broadcast, the announcer would key into a keyboard a number unique to the company that the next news item was about. This unique number would be broadcast digitally prior to the news announcement. Your box would see the code and, if it matched one of your companies of interest, the box would turn on, allowing you to hear the announcement.

Dow Jones spent a lot on this service and launched it. It failed miserably. There was no need.

THE FIRST MBA DIRECTIVE IS PURPOSE

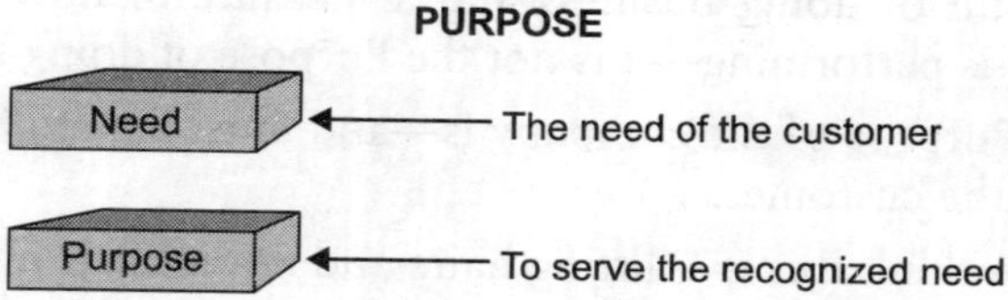

The first Directive in Mission-Based Alignment is the company's Purpose—a simple, one-sentence statement of the recognized customer need and how the company will fill that need. Despite what many executives and business school professors might say, it is not the primary purpose of a company to make money or "enhance shareholder value".

There is an interesting phenomenon in business. Companies who focus on making money and enhancing shareholder value don't accomplish either—at least not very well. However, companies who focus on serving the needs of the customer make attractive returns, produce net cash, and maximize shareholder value.

Don't misunderstand. Financial strength is vital if a company is to survive, thrive, and grow. Financial strength is important for several reasons:

- If a company has financial strength and positive cash flow (at least from operations), it controls its own destiny. If it doesn't produce net cash, others control its destiny.
- Financial strength allows a company to remain independent, if it chooses to do so.
- Financial strength provides leverage for acquisitions, if they make sense.
- Financial strength provides flexibility to react quickly to changing customer needs.
- Financial strength allows founders, investors, and key employees to reap the rewards of their risk and efforts without ceding control to others.

However, making a profit (or enhancing shareholder value) is the result of doing business and a measure of how well the company is performing—it is not the Purpose of doing business.

The Purpose of the company is—and must be—to fulfill the needs of the customer.

If you think this is splitting hairs and not all that important, take a look at Steelcase. This company dominated the modular office furniture market, an industry that took off when office cubicles became popular. Although many competitors offered similar systems at considerably lower prices, Steelcase continued to lead the industry in virtually every category. This was when the company was privately held. Then, the company went public, and the wheels came off.

From the outside looking in, it appears that their Purpose changed. After their IPO, they seem to have believed that their Purpose was now to "enhance shareholder value". As we will discuss in more depth later on, the signals that top management sends throughout the company establish the company's agenda and priorities in the minds of the employees. If the employees on the front line believe that profits have now surpassed serving the customer in priority, they will adjust their actions and decisions accordingly. This can lead to disaster.

Another company who made a similar mistake was Boeing. However, unlike Steelcase, Boeing's previous priorities were also flawed. We will discuss Boeing later, since prior to the current leadership, this company was a classic example of non-alignment.

Secondly, the Purpose must not be to pursue a technology. Technology is only viable and valuable to the extent that it fulfills some need of a customer. Technology for its own sake will not win.

Tacan, a company headquartered in Carlsbad, California, has been involved in fiber optic technology for over ten years. Yet, the company has never focused on any specific customer need. As a result, they have languished while others in fiber optics soared.

It is also not the Purpose of the company to beat the competition. Beating the competition—like profits and higher market capitalization—is the result of adhering to the Seven Guiding Principles by implementing MBA, thereby raising the bar of performance in your company. If you serve your customer better, know better where that customer's need is going, and get there first, you will become the competitor to beat. You will be the leader. Those trying to beat the competition will forever be followers, waiting to see where and how the competition moves and then reacting and responding to those moves.

Think of Purpose in the following way. What is the central theme of management discussions? What is the central focus? What does the leader go to bed and wake up thinking about? What issue creates a persistent sense of urgency in the leaders, managers and employees?

In order to follow the First Principle, central focus and sense of urgency must always be on the customer and his/her need. Other issues, while important, are secondary.

PRINCIPLE #2: THE MISSION MUST *IDENTIFY* THE CUSTOMER

As you might expect, the company's Mission, which is the second Directive, is the central tenet of Mission-Based Alignment. Three of the Seven Principles deal with the Mission.

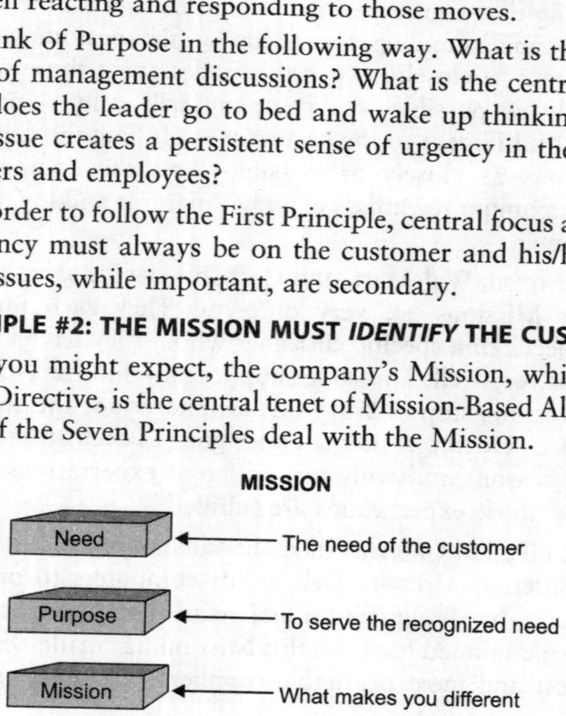

The Mission is the guts of Mission-Based Alignment. This is not the mission statement you see framed and hanging in the lobby of many companies—a mission that says, in essence, "We will be the best at what we do, and our employees are our most important asset." In Mission-Based Alignment, the Mission Statement is a well thought out, hard-hitting statement of:

- Who the customer is;
- What that customer expects from the company;
- What specific product(s) or service(s) the company will deliver to the customer;
- How the product(s) or service(s) will be delivered; and
- How the company will be different from the other companies who offer to serve that customer.

In its Mission Statement, the company chooses its customers by selecting that segment of the overall market that it elects to serve. By understanding the needs of the customers within that segment as closely as possible and serving those needs as completely as possible, the company will deliver maximum value and fulfillment to the customer—fulfilling the customer's expectations as closely as possible—and the company will receive maximum rewards; i.e. higher margins and loyalty from the customer.

Nordstrom, Wal-Mart, and CostCo have the same purpose, but their Missions are very different. They each target the specific needs of a specific customer whom they have identified and know very well. The same shopper may shop at Nordstrom in the morning, stop at Wal-Mart around noon, and then head for CostCo. However, that shopper goes to each store for very different reasons and with very different expectations. And in each case, those expectations are fulfilled.

Dell, HP, and Gateway have the same purpose, but Dell has a very different Mission. Dell builds computers to order and sells direct—bypassing traditional retail distribution channels, and a single-minded focus on this Mission has made Dell one of the largest and most profitable suppliers of computers in the world.

PRINCIPLE #3: THE MISSION MUST DIFFERENTIATE HOW THE COMPANY WILL SERVE THE CUSTOMER NEED IN WAYS THAT HAVE REAL VALUE TO THE CUSTOMER

Differentiation is vital. In the final analysis, there are two—and only two—strategies from which a company can choose if it wants to thrive, grow, and control its destiny. It can choose to be the low cost competitor in its geographic market(s), or it can clearly differentiate itself from its competitors. If a company does neither and attempts to be "all things to all people", it will find itself, like K-Mart, caught in the middle.

Top performing companies clearly differentiate themselves in ways that are important to the customer. Customers have very clear expectations when they do business with these winners and those expectations are consistently fulfilled. By intensely focusing on the need of specific customers, these companies, such as Dell, Wal-Mart, Nordstrom, and FedEx, are, in effect, choosing their customers.

If you don't choose your customers, then your customers will choose you with needs that are diverse enough to keep you from maximizing value or clearly differentiating yourself from your competitors. This is often the main area where young companies falter. In a short-term effort to increase sales, they accept orders for products or services that depart from the product or service they intended to provide.

Appian Graphics is a young company that designs and manufactures video accelerator cards for personal computers. These printed circuit cards and accompanying software extend a single Windows desktop onto two or more video displays at the same time, allowing a user to, for example, have a Word document on one screen and an Excel spreadsheet on another with the ability to cut-and-paste from one to the other by simply moving the mouse. This is a powerful feature with many apparent and compelling uses. Appian Graphics agreed to a contract with a Japanese flat panel TV manufacturer to use Appian Graphics' core technology to produce a video card for the new "thin" TV. The Japanese company paid for the R&D to adapt the technology for their particular need. The contract will produce sales for Appian Graphics. However, the Japanese TV manufacturer owns the rights to the TV technology (since they paid for it). Much technical and management talent will be drained to fulfill this contract; yet it does not fulfill the Mission and does not move Appian Graphics towards its Vision. Appian Graphics should have politely declined the opportunity.

If you don't differentiate, your only other option is to become the low cost producer. There can be only one low cost producer (low *cost*—not low *price*!) in any geographic market and maintaining that position can be difficult. Just ask K-Mart or Woolworth, both of whom did fine until Wal-Mart, Sam's Club, and CostCo came along. Toys R Us, a traditional low cost producer, failed to detect a change in the customer need—a change toward increasing demand for customer service.

PRINCIPLE #4: THE MISSION MUST CONTAIN PRIORITIZED VALUES THAT TRULY REFLECT THE BUSINESS VALUES OF THE COMPANY'S LEADERSHIP

The Mission defines who the customer is, what the company will do for that customer, and how the company will do those things differently than its competitors. The Mission also defines and prioritizes the company's values and principles. Values and principles are important to a company and its employees. Values and principles tell the employees what is important to the company, how the company will conduct itself on a day-to-day basis, and how the company expects its employees to conduct themselves.

The values should be well thought out and must reflect the true view of the company's executive management towards the business, the customer, the employees, the owners, and the community. The true test of values comes when the decision to stick with them is tough. If they are ever violated, it would have been better for the company to never have issued them in the first place.

Companies should always include the following two concepts in their statement of values:

- We will not make commitments to our customers, our employees, and our owners that we cannot keep, and we will keep the commitments we make; and
- We value, respect, and trust our customers, employees, and owners, and we will strive everyday to earn and deserve their respect and trust.

Most employees develop very keen BS detectors early in their working careers. Everything executives do and say—how they spend their time, what decisions they make, what makes them frown and what makes them smile—must be in line with and consistent with the Mission and its stated values—100% of the time. Once trust is lost, it takes a long time to rebuild it.

The values must also be prioritized. Many apparent conflicts exist in business. Quality vs. profit. Pleasing the customer vs. profit. Believing the customer vs. believing the employee. Values should be prioritized, and a "higher" value should never be violated in fulfillment of a "lower" value.

One of the keys to Mission-Based Alignment is the constant preaching of the Mission and values to all employees at every opportunity. Once they understand and embrace the Mission and the prioritized values, the employees will then (and only then) have the knowledge they need to make day-to-day decisions that are in tune with the Mission without the necessity of checking with a manager. This is true empowerment and is an essential ingredient of the company's success.

PRINCIPLE #5: ALL DIRECTIVES OF THE COMPANY MUST BE BROUGHT IN LINE WITH THE PURPOSE AND THE MISSION

VISION

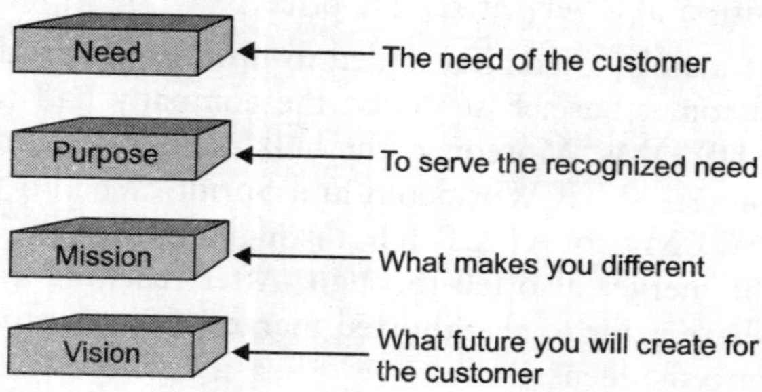

In Mission-Based Alignment, we have segmented the functions or activities of a company into 7 Directives—Purpose, Mission, Vision, Strategy, Structure, Systems, and Performance. To facilitate discussion and understanding, we have listed these Directives separately. As we will discuss later, they are, in fact, intermingled and interdependent.

In top performing companies, these Directives are consistent with and in alignment with each other. We have already discussed the first two Directives—Purpose and Mission.

After the Mission comes the Vision—what the company will do in the future for the customer. Vision can be tricky. When a company is small, it should be a "one trick pony"—find one specific customer need, understand that need as much as possible, and fill that need as closely as possible.

Compaq Computer (which has since been acquired by HP) began by making the first, durable portable PC. (Actually, their first product is better described as "luggable" rather than portable.) Soon, they got better at it and thrived. Later, as the company matured, it broadened its product line.

Ciena makes devices called Dense Wavelength Division Multiplexers (DWDMs). These products allow a telecommunications company to send many different signals over a single fiber optic circuit. DWDMs fulfilled a very real need for companies such as MCI Worldcom and Sprint, as telecommunications traffic, fueled by fax machines, cell phones, and ultimately, the Internet, grew much faster than had been projected. Ciena grew very rapidly and was courted by Tellabs for acquisition at a very attractive price.

Unfortunately, Ciena had failed to broaden its product line and its customer base. Essentially, the company had only one product—DWDMs. Moreover, the bulk of its sales came from two customers—MCI Worldcom and Sprint. When a possible sale of DWDMs to AT&T fell through at literally the last second, the merger also fell through. After reaching a price of $96 per share prior to the aborted merger, Ciena's stock price plunged into the teens.

Vision must include the broadening of products, customer base, and geography. Wanting to do these things is easy. Knowing when to do them is the tricky part.

Before it was acquired by HP, Compaq had moved way beyond the portable computer to providing a full range of computers and related products, such as servers. Dell has also expanded its product portfolio. Once the customer has developed a loyalty based on continuous positive experiences of doing business with a company, they are willing (and often eager) to buy other related products or services from that company.

However, while expanding horizontally, vertically, and/or geographically, a company must be especially careful not to jeopardize its alignment and those things that got it to where it is. This is why acquisitions can be so tricky and, too often, don't work. Many times, an acquisition prospect has alignment problems, which is why it is available at anything approaching a reasonable price in the first place. If an unaligned company is acquired, it is essential that it be brought into alignment ASAP, before it infects its aligned parent.

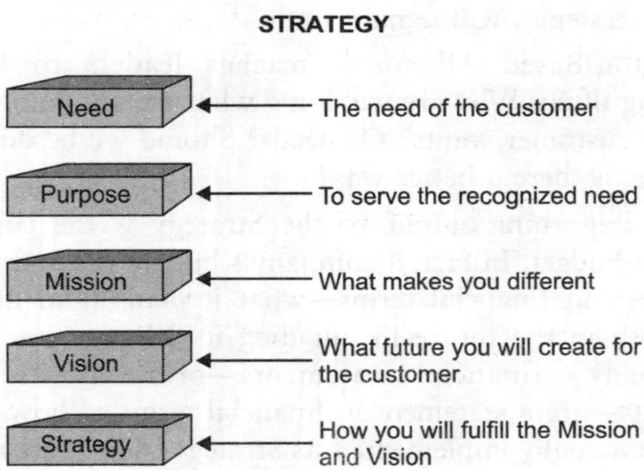

After the Mission/Vision comes the Strategy, a detailed plan of how the company will execute the Mission and make the Vision happen. The Strategy defines who will do what, by when, and with what resources to realize the Mission/Vision.

Before Jack Welch took the helm at General Electric, the company was languishing. Its sales grew annually about the same percentage as the GNP. Profits were "okay". Many analysts believed that the company was so big that it couldn't grow much faster than it did.

Welch had a different plan and a different Mission. In order to fulfill the Mission, he decreed that GE would not participate in any businesses in which it did not have (or couldn't attain) the number one or two market share. In order to realize this Mission, GE exited many of the businesses it was in. Because it is a very large company, GE tended to focus on businesses where size matters, leveraging the company's size and financial muscle. Sales and profits began a healthy growth.

When many companies develop their "business plan", they begin with Strategy. In doing so, they sometimes commit two fundamental errors:

- They assume that the path they are on is the right path, and
- They assume that their competitors' positions and strategies will remain static.

Mission-Based Alignment teaches leaders to question everything often. Why are we doing what we are doing? Is this what the customer wants? Or needs? Should we be doing it at all? If yes, is there a better way?

One important output of the Strategy is the company's operating budget. In fact, a company's budget is a statement of its Strategy in financial terms—what it plans (and hopes) to accomplish in the future in pursuing its Mission and Vision. A company's financial statements—primarily its income statements—are a statement in financial terms of how well (or poorly) it actually implemented its Strategy in the past and how well the Strategy was aligned with the Mission in the first place.

Taken together, the Mission, Vision and Strategy constitute the Leadership Directives and are the responsibility of the company's leadership—primarily the CEO. By carefully developing a comprehensive, customer- and company-specific Mission and preaching that Mission at every opportunity throughout the company, the leadership of the company is freed from day-to-day micro-management and is now able to monitor and refine the Mission, so that the company and the Mission remain in tune with the ever changing need of the customer.

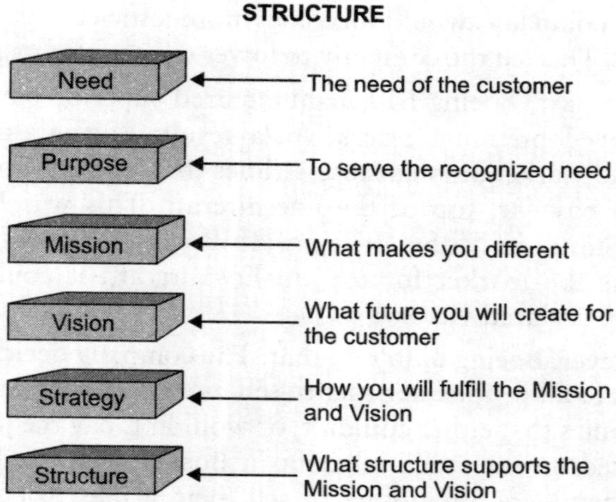

Next comes the Structure, which defines—usually in writing—how the company is organized and how it operates. Structure includes (but is not limited to) the business financial model, the business plan, the budget, employee manuals or handbooks, organizational charts, compensation plans, training manuals, training curricula, quality programs, policies and procedures.

A few years ago, Boeing had many problems. (Obviously, if you achieve a 60% share of a large global market and you lose millions in the process, it goes without saying that you have problems.) If you turn back to the beginning of this book and review the symptoms of non-alignment, those symptoms described Boeing a few years ago.

For several years, Boeing's Mission was to increase its market share. (There are subtle but important differences between Boeing's Mission and GE's Mission.) Besides the fact that this Mission does not respond to a Customer Need (the customer could care less what your market share is), the rest of Boeing's Directives were not in alignment with the Mission. One of the elements of Structure is the financial business model a company uses to guide decision-making and the day-to-day management of the company. Boeing's financial model assumed that the company would become more efficient as volume increased. This led the company to lower the price of its aircraft.

In the past, Boeing had manufactured superior planes and had received premium prices. As a result, Boeing essentially owned the market among those airlines that wanted, and could afford to pay for, top of the line aircraft. This was Boeing's customer and its differentiation. If Boeing had defined its market as the market for top quality aircraft, it could have, rightfully, declared victory.

However, Boeing didn't do that. The company decided to be all things to all people. In order to sell more planes, it had to sell to companies that either couldn't, or wouldn't, pay the premium price based on the value inherent in Boeing's planes. In other words, they were attempting to sell their planes to customers who did not necessarily want the value that had been recognized and sought by Boeing's traditional customers.

Imagine that Nordstrom decides to increase its market share by going after J.C. Penney's customers. While maintaining its high level of service and product quality, Nordstrom slashes prices, drawing in Penney's customers but losing its shirt in the process.

As implausible as that might sound, it is exactly what Boeing did. The company cut prices without cutting costs. Their financial model and other parts of the company's Structure and Systems were not in alignment with the Mission. The more planes the company assembled and sold, the more money it lost.

Boeing then changed its Mission to "enhancing shareholder value". In doing so, they replaced one bad Mission with another bad Mission.

The financial model and the budget must accurately reflect the dynamics of operating the business in line with the Mission and in pursuit of the Vision. Both must in essence be a financial statement of the Strategy, since budgets contain the dimensions of time and resources.

In Mission-Based Alignment, there is a clear distinction between frugality and cheapness. The frugal company does not waste. Mission-Based Alignment clearly exposes those activities within the company which are not in alignment with the Mission. Once identified, these activities are eliminated, removing waste and creating true savings.

The cheap company, on the other hand, attempts not to pay full value for those resources it needs to fulfill its Mission. This in itself is anti-alignment and, while possibly producing short-term savings, serves as a large obstacle in the path of fulfillling the Mission.

Companies who have downsized for the wrong reasons have discovered that this type of savings is illusory at best and, in fact, can cripple the company in its efforts to thrive and grow by serving the customer need. Budgets which are derived from and are in alignment with Mission-Based financial models and dynamics cannot be "trimmed" without creating a negative effect on the Mission.

Likewise, all the other elements of Structure must be in line with the Mission. The structure of the organization itself—the org chart—should be driven by the customer need and the optimal structure to fulfill that need. Companies sometimes organize around personalities. However, no one person transcends the Mission. The employees must adapt to the Mission. You cannot adapt the Mission to the employee, because the Mission focuses on the customer and the customer does not care about the individuals in the company. The customer cares only about how responsive the company is to his or her need.

The Structure of the company is the skeleton of the organism. It provides the framework within which employees fulfill the need of the customer. Every element of the company, particularly the Structure, must be continuously examined to uncover the obstacles that lie between the employee and the fulfillment of the Mission. Once detected, the obstacles must be rooted out.

All of the elements of Structure must be in tune with the Mission. If not, Structure—not Mission—will define and guide the employees' day-to-day actions and decisions.

SYSTEMS

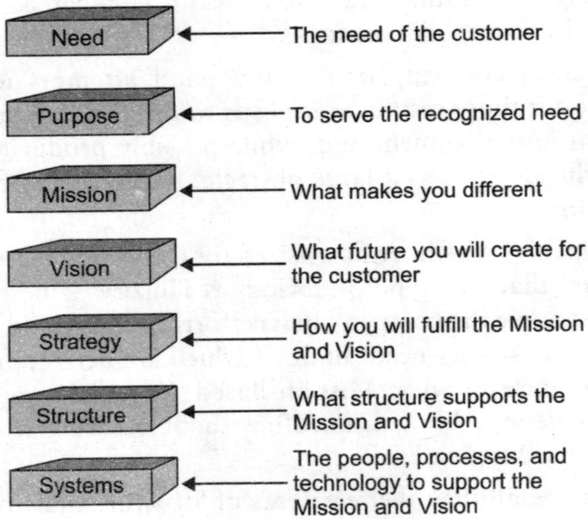

After Structure, we have Systems—the people, technology, and processes that, together, produce the products or define and deliver the services. This is where the "rubber meets the road" and where most of the time, energy, and money of the company are invested.

In a manufacturing company, the Systems include the assembly workers and all of the technology and processes that bring in the parts, distribute them to the floor, track the products through the manufacturing cycle, inspect the finished products, transfer the products to inventory, and eventually ship the products to the customer. It also includes all of the tools, test equipment, machinery, and other technology used by the workers to manufacture and test the products as well as to track and control the flow of material on the manufacturing floor.

The Systems must be in tune with the manufacturing strategy, which itself must support the Mission. A company can design to order, make to order, make to forecast, or make to inventory. Which manufacturing strategy the company selects must be in response to the customer's need and the company's

Mission, and all other Directives must be in alignment with this manufacturing strategy.

In a service business, such as fast food, the actual restaurants themselves are the Systems—the employees who take the order and prepare and serve the food along with the processes and technology they use to take and record the order, control inventories, ensure quality, and prepare and deliver the food as ordered.

Wendy's implemented a strategy of cooking and preparing their hamburgers to order, rather than cooking them in advance and keeping them warm until sold. Wendy's had identified an unfilled need. When Wendy's entered the market, there were three large players—McDonald's, Burger King, and Burger Chef. The prevailing wisdom at the time said that there wasn't room for another nationwide hamburger fast food company. Wendy's made room by fulfilling an identified, unmet need and displaced Burger Chef, who faded and disappeared.

Regardless of the actions of executives and managers, the customer need is either met or not met by the Systems. If the employees do not know about, understand, and embrace the Mission, there is no hope of maximizing the customer's reward by meeting his/her need and expectations as closely as possible.

Process re-engineering and technology upgrades take place at the Systems level. As you can now see, if the processes and technology are not aligned with the higher directives of Mission, Vision, Strategy, and Structure, then all of the improvements and upgrades in the world won't help. They will still be the wrong processes and technology. Only now, the investment in them will be higher.

Systems also must be horizontally aligned—aligned among themselves. The people, processes, and technology must be balanced. During the '90's, too many companies concentrated on advancements in technology—both manufacturing and computer technology—without commensurate advancements in processes or increased training for the people who use the technology. The weakest link analogy works here. Systems will be no better and no more effective than its weakest component.

After Systems, we have Performance, the output of the Systems. Performance is the product or service that is delivered to and perceived by the customer. This is the face of the company that the customer sees—its products/services, the people who answer the phone at order input or customer service, the sales people, the brochures and other printed material, the investor relations communications. These day-to-day, minute-by-minute encounters with various company employees establish the perception of the company in the mind of the customer. If they are all aligned one to another and all are focused on meeting the need of the customer that the company has selected to serve, the perception of the customer will be very positive and the customer will return time and time again, regardless (within a broad range) of the price.

The Structure and Systems constitute the Management Directives and are the responsibility of Management. In a sense, the Leadership is concerned that the company is doing the right things, while the Management is concerned that the company is doing those things right. By aligning the Structure and the Systems with the Mission/Vision and Strategies, Management ensures that it is removing the obstacles that stand in the way of the employees following and fulfilling the Mission and delivering precisely what the customer needs.

When all of these elements are in close alignment, the company focuses its time and energy on meeting the needs of the customer and avoids wasteful uses of resources that are not in line with the Mission. Also, by effectively communicating the Mission throughout the company, Leadership gives the employees the information they need—empowers them, if you will—to make the day-to-day decisions that are in tune with the Mission without having to rely on Management to make every decision. This frees Leadership to focus on the Mission and lead, and it frees Management to focus on the Structure and Systems, insuring that they remain aligned with the Mission.

THE ALIGNED BUSINESS

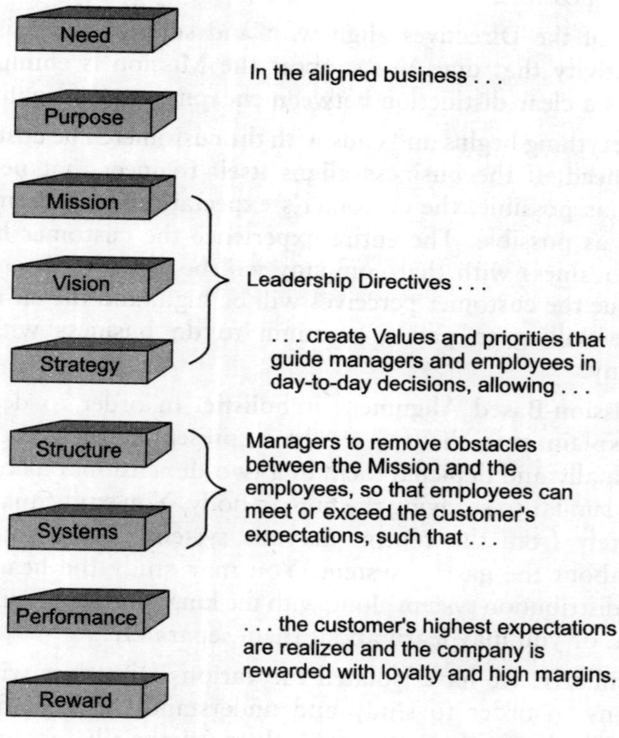

In the aligned company, Leadership and Management have different responsibilities.

- Leadership recognizes and understands the customer need, nurtures the Mission to fulfill that need in a way that differentiates the company in the eyes of the customer, and ensures that the Strategy makes the Mission happen. Leadership focuses religiously on the Mission and preaches it constantly to all employees.
- Management ensures that the Structure and Systems are balanced among themselves and in alignment with all higher Directives, especially the Mission. Management also identifies and removes the obstacles that stand in the way of the employees fulfilling the

Mission and meeting the customer need as closely as possible.

All of the Directives align with and support the Mission. Any activity that does not support the Mission is eliminated. There is a clear distinction between cheapness and frugality.

Everything begins and ends with the customer. The customer has a need. If the business aligns itself to meet that need as closely as possible, the customer's expectations will be met as closely as possible. The entire experience the customer has of doing business with that company will be positive. Therefore, the value the customer perceives will be high, and the customer will be willing to pay a premium to do business with the company.

Mission-Based Alignment is holistic. In order to describe and explain this theory, we have presented the Directives individually and depicted them in a two-dimensional hierarchy. This is similar to studying the human body. You study anatomy, separately from the central nervous system. Then, you may learn about the gastric system. You may study the heart and blood distribution system along with the lungs and the respiratory system, or you may learn about them separately.

Similarly, we have isolated the various Directives within a company in order to study and understand the dynamics of each. We have also presented them pictorially as existing separately in a hierarchy that begins with the Customer Need and ends with Performance and the Customer Reward.

All of the Directives are in fact intertwined and interrelated in a three dimensional sphere that is surrounded by the customer. Every element flows into and derives output from every other element. Information, knowledge, and understanding must flow seamlessly and without interruption throughout the company, from the CEO to the production line worker. Everything that happens—all decisions, all communications, all activities, all spending—must be in alignment and harmony with the Mission and the Vision.

MBA is Holistic

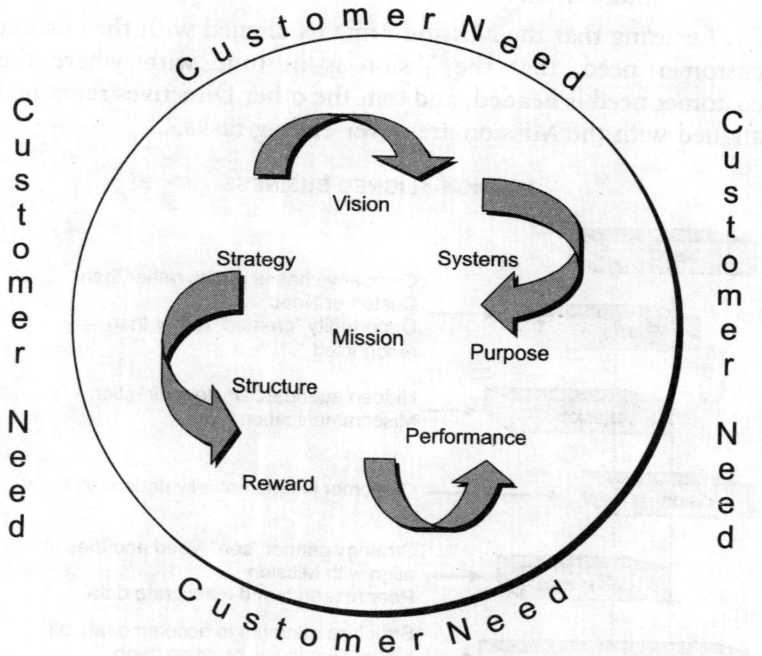

Perfect alignment is unattainable. The Company is either moving towards or away from alignment.

- Customer needs change.
- An aligned company will grow. It can't help but grow. Growth means additional employees who don't yet know or embrace the Mission. Growth means new processes and new technology.
- Tough decisions must be made. If the Values are compromised, alignment slips.
- Conflicts can arise between the discipline required to adhere to the Mission and the creativity of many employees. Creativity is vital to the company in detecting and adjusting to changes in Customer Need. The challenge of leaders and managers is to channel

creativity into areas that are aligned with the Mission and Vision.

Ensuring that the Mission remains aligned with the current customer need, that the Vision is in tune with where the customer need is headed, and that the other Directives remained aligned with the Mission are never-ending tasks.

THE NON-ALIGNED BUSINESS

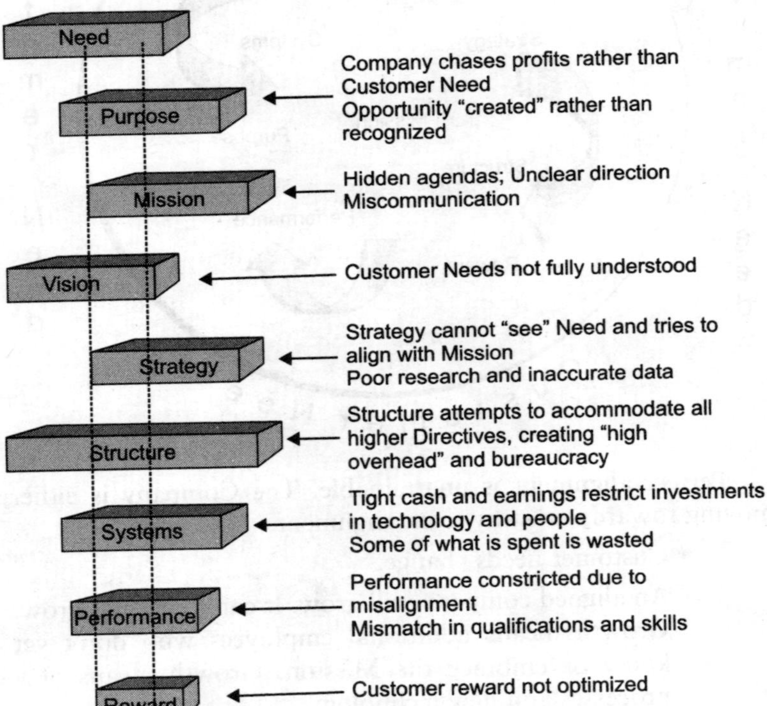

As you can see from the diagram, if the Directives are not aligned, the focus is lost, resources are squandered, and, worst of all, the needs of the customer are only partially met, resulting in low margins, tight cash, missed projections, employee frustration, and poor performance.

We can look upon the customer need as the "zone of opportunity" for the company:

- All planning, decisions, and activities that take place within the zone contribute to fulfilling the customer need.
- All planning, decisions, and activities that take place outside of the zone are at best a waste of resources and at worse a dilution and defocus of the Mission.

Purpose can get out of alignment if the company sees its Purpose as making money (Boeing—Steelcase). It will also be out of alignment if the company is creating a need or focusing on a technology rather than recognizing a customer need (Apple's Newton). If any portion of the Purpose is out of alignment, that effort is not addressing a customer need and therefore is expended in areas where there are no customers.

Non-aligned Missions result from multiple agendas, unclear directions, miscommunication (or no communication), or failure to differentiate (K-Mart). Those efforts outside of the zone of opportunity address the wrong customers—those customers who, for whatever reasons, cannot or will not recognize and reward the value inherent in the company's efforts.

Vision alignment problems arise from not fully understanding the customer need and where that need is headed. The result is that the company moves in the wrong direction or doesn't move at all (Ciena—Toys R Us).

If the Mission is out of Alignment, the Strategy will also be out of alignment because it tries to align itself with the Mission. This leads to an ineffective plan (Boeing).

If higher Directives are not in alignment, then Structure, by its very nature, "widens" to accommodate all higher Directives. This produces costs and efforts well outside of the zone of opportunity, creates bureaucracy (which, since it is not clearly focused on an identified customer need, begins to exist for its own purposes), and results in overheads that the business dynamics cannot support (Boeing).

At this point, Systems cannot clearly see any direction. It therefore uses history ("that's the way we do things around here") as its guide and justification for its plans, decisions, and efforts—perpetuating non-alignment and moving even further from changing customer needs (Toys R Us—Boeing).

Different companies are driven by different forces. They may be:

- Earnings Driven
- Asset Driven
- Inventory Driven
- Manufacturing Driven
- Expense Driven
- Owner Driven

Mission-Based companies who align the elements of the organization are Customer Driven, and these are the companies who continually rank at the top of their industry.

The Keys to Success

There are several keys which are vital in managing for success through the implementation and practice of Mission-Based Alignment.

Customer Need

Leadership must be in tune with the customer and his/her need. There is an important difference between customers and markets.

- Markets don't exist; customers do. Markets are merely a convenient way to amalgamate groups of customers who make independent buying decisions for a variety of reasons. Moreover, the groupings can be defined in such a way to tell any story you want to tell. In Mission-Based Alignment, the target market represents those customers who will place the highest value on the company's differentiation. In developing its business model and strategy, it is obviously important that the target market be large enough to support the company's growth and provide the financial support to achieve its goals and fuel future growth and profitability. A target market that is too small will not sustain the company. Conversely, a target market that is too large may not respond favorably to the company's differentiation.
- Markets don't buy anything; Customers do. Individual customers make independent buying decisions. We cannot understand and respond to the needs of a

market, because a market doesn't have needs. Only customers have needs that the successful company will recognize and fulfill.

- Customer needs change in real time. Market trends reveal after the fact that the customer needs began to change at some point in time in the past.

The Leadership must get past market numbers and get to know the customer and his need. This usually means spending sufficient time "in the field" "touching" the customer; finding out what "floats his or her boat". This task cannot be delegated to the sales force. The job of the sales force is to sell the products or services that the company currently provides. The responsibility of the Leadership is to insure that those products or services remain aligned with the customer need.

Not only does the customer need change; sometimes that change can be sudden and significant. Earlier, we discussed the natural gross margin range of a product or service. In this concept, customers will pay more or less for a product or service within a certain range based on how well that product or service fulfills their need and expectation; e.g. how much value they place on the product or service and the total experience of doing business with the company providing the product or service.

However, that margin range can move. For example, over the past five to ten years, we have seen a significant lowering in the margin range of personal computers. This change was caused by a growing realization that computer hardware was largely the same in performance and reliability, regardless of which company provided it. The mystique had been removed, and personal computers became more of a commodity. A margin range continues to exist; the top end of the margin range has simply moved downward.

Companies who failed to detect this trend early enough were caught with bloated inventories and no new lower cost products. By the time they detected the movement by watching the market trend, it was too late. Those companies, such as Dell, who kept in touch with the customer detected the trend as it was happening.

PRINCIPLE #6: THE LEADER MUST PREACH THE MISSION THROUGHOUT THE COMPANY WITH A RELIGIOUS-LIKE ZEAL AND COMMITMENT

Leadership

The roles of leaders and managers in the company are distinctly different. One of the many key aspects of Mission-Based Alignment is that by defining and communicating the Mission and values throughout the company and thereby empowering the Managers and employees to make day-to-day decisions aligned with the Mission, Leadership is freed from micro-management and is now able to lead.

The Late Admiral Grace Hopper was in her time the highest-ranking woman in the Navy. She is also credited with developing a leading computer programing language—COBOL. More important to us, she understood the difference between management and leadership. She said the following:

> "You cannot manage a man into combat, you must lead him. You manage things, you lead people."
>
> "While excellent management requires the most extensive understanding of processes to be managed, excellent leadership requires the most extensive understanding of people to be led."
>
> "Managers try to do things right. Leaders try to do the right things."

Leadership's job is to keep the organization focused on accomplishing the Mission, while ensuring that the Mission is the right Mission. Management's job is to eliminate the barriers to accomplishing the Mission, implementing the Strategies, and providing the Structure for the workers to responsively accomplish the Mission, using processes designed to optimize effectiveness and technology fitted to optimize efficiency. While Leadership is responsible for the development of the Mission and the Strategy, Management is responsible for the development of the Structure and the Systems necessary to implement the Mission and the Strategy.

Some believe that leaders are born, not made. On the other hand, there is a thriving industry devoted to Leadership Training.

There are several skills or personality profiling systems available to help gauge an individual's aptitude towards effective leadership. Our favorite is the MBTI.

The Myers-Briggs Type Indicator (MBTI), a personality topography based on the work of Carl Jung, defines 16 different personality types. Within these personality types, some are predisposed towards becoming leaders and others are not. This fact has several implications for companies.

First, using MBTI (or a similar methodology) to better understand and know the managers within an organization would be one important factor in determining who should be placed on a track to rise to positions of formal leadership. Perhaps more importantly, an organization's structure should allow "natural" leaders to surface. Given half a chance, they will surface. Denied that chance, they will usually leave. On the other hand, whether or not a person's MBTI predisposes him or her towards leadership, anyone will become a better leader with leadership training than without it.

As the guardian of the company's values, it is vital that the Leader's actions be in synch with the company's values 100% of the time. The effectiveness of Leaders is dependent on their ability to recognize the distant horizon (Vision), determine the point of convergence (Purpose and Mission), chart the course (Strategy) and communicate to the followers. By communicating the company's directives in a simple, clear, and consistent manner, the objective is never in doubt. Each and every employee is then empowered to succeed by acting on behalf of the customer within the boundaries of the Mission and the prioritized values and requires little or no supervision.

With the training and empowerment of the employees, Management is free to "eliminate the barriers" that prevent those employees from delivering on the Mission. These barriers may include non-aligned Structure, Processes or Technology, skill enhancement, resources, mentoring, coaching, and conflict resolution.

Communications

Having determined the customer need and developed the Mission which states how the company will fulfill that need in ways that are different, thereby increasing the value to the customer of doing business with the company, Leadership must communicate the Mission throughout the company.

The Mission must take on religious aspects, and the Leader must communicate the Mission with an intensity approaching religious fervor. One of the keys to Mission-Based Alignment is the constant preaching of the Mission and values to all employees at every opportunity. Once they understand and embrace the Mission and the prioritized values, the employees will then (and only then) have the knowledge they need to make day-to-day decisions that are in tune with the Mission without the necessity of checking with a manager. This is true empowerment and is an essential ingredient of the company's success.

We want to repeat this. We have seen top executives hold an all-too-infrequent meeting with employees and talk about financial measures, such as margins, profits, and inventory turns. This is a major mistake for three reasons:

- Employees don't understand and don't care about such matters, because they generally don't understand the financial dynamics of the business, and, to the extent that they do understand, they don't feel that, individually, they can affect these results (and they are right).
- These types of meetings turn the employees "off" to the prospect of employee meetings.
- These types of meetings squander a valuable chance to talk about the customer and the Mission, things the employee can relate to.

Leaders must have a deep sense of who the company is, where it is going, and how it is going to get there. They must then constantly communicate this message to the troops at every opportunity. If Leaders do this without let-up, the company just might win. If they don't, the company doesn't have a prayer.

PRINCIPLE #7: EVERY EMPLOYEE, INCLUDING THE CEO, MUST SUBORDINATE HIS/HER NEEDS TO THE NEEDS OF THE COMPANY

Early on, at the time of start-up and for a while thereafter, the company does not have an existence in and of itself. True, it is a group of people (or maybe just one) who have joined together for a common purpose. But during this period, the company can die quickly (over a weekend), if, for example, key people depart.

At some point, though, the company takes on a life of its own. It becomes a separate, "living" entity. The people can leave; the location can change; even the products and/or services it provides can change. But the company survives. If death does come, it comes slowly.

It is often difficult to know when this "birth" occurs. However, we do know that it occurs, at the latest, when the company reaches sustained operational positive cash flow or when the company takes on significant debt (whichever comes first).

Why is this concept important? Because after the company is "born", it is imperative that every employee—from the CEO on down—subordinate his or her needs to the needs of the business. **Without this subordination of needs by all employees, differing agendas will arise and misalignment will inevitably follow.**

Where does the competition fit into all this? In case you haven't noticed, we haven't stressed competitors very much. Sure, it's important to know and understand what the competition is doing and where they are heading. However, too many executives become fixated on the competition. It becomes their central focus, and they spend too much time and energy responding to the competition.

If you are forever responding to the competition, you are letting them define the game. They are the ones breaking new ground and finding new ways to meet the customer need, and you are always following; always behind; always late.

If you align your company with a truly differentiated Mission focused on fulfilling the customer need, you set the pace. You become the competitor to emulate. You are out front. You become the one to beat.

Implementation and Measuring

3

Let's restate the 7 Guiding Principles in MBA terminology. The 7 Guiding Principles believed in and adhered to by companies who attain and sustain a position at the top of their industry and consistently exhibit exceptional performance and produce exceptional results are:

1. The Purpose of a Company is to serve a recognized Customer Need.
   - Profit is a measure of the Company's performance, not its Purpose
   - Beating the competition is the result of alignment
   - The Purpose must be based on customer need, not technology
   - The customer need must be real, not in the mind of the company
2. The Mission must identify the customer.
   - The company must address customers who will recognize and reward the company's differentiation
   - Attempting to be "all things to all people" will dilute the differentiation to the point that the value is eliminated and price alone becomes the determining factor
3. The Mission must differentiate how it will serve the customer need in ways that have real value to the customer.
4. The Mission must contain prioritized values that truly reflect the business values of the leader.
   - The values must be followed without exception

- No higher value can be compromised in pursuit of a lower value

5. All Directives of the company must be brought in line with the Purpose and the Mission.
6. The Leader must preach the Mission throughout the company with a religious-like zeal and commitment.
   - All employees must buy into the Mission.
   - Understanding and acceptance of the Mission must be obtained from the top down—in that order.
7. Every employee, including the CEO, must subordinate his/her needs to the needs of the company.

BALANCED SCORECARD

Perfect Alignment is an unattainable goal, which leadership must constantly strive to approach. All organizations are continually moving towards, or away from, alignment.

After the theory, methodology and tools of Mission-Based Alignment have been put in place, the company should establish four sets of metrics, referred to as a "balanced scorecard", in order to monitor its progress and detect trends towards non-alignment as soon as possible so that early, corrective action can be taken.

Most companies rely on financial results to guide their performance and to institute corrective actions. While financial results are the first element of the balanced scorecard, they are, in fact, the most lagging indicators in the scorecard. It sometimes takes a few months for waste, once identified and "eliminated", to wash its way through the company's financial statements. Also, trends have inertia. Alignment improvements must first slow and then reverse negative trends. Relying solely on past financial results is like steering a boat by watching its wake.

Many companies also track quality, which is the second element of the balanced scorecard. Quality measures are also lagging indicators, but they do reflect more recent trends than are indicated in financial statements.

In many companies, "quality" means the MTBF (mean time between failures) of a product. In Mission-Based Alignment, quality means everything that the Company does that "touches" the Customer—things such as the product or service itself, the total responsiveness of the customer service personnel to customer inquiries (not merely answering the phone within 3 rings), the customer friendliness of the invoice and the responsiveness of the accounting department to billing inquiries, and the helpfulness and truthfulness of sales personnel.

Quality must be quantified and measured constantly. If quality trends begin to slow (or turn negative), the company is already moving away from alignment.

The third part of the balanced scorecard includes customer complaints and attitudes. While many companies pay attention to complaints, few have a structured, systematic way of tracking customer attitudes and their trends on a consistent, ongoing basis. Customer attitudes are a current indicator. A consistent, objective method for quantifying and tracking customer attitudes must be developed and implemented. This is a touchy process, because simply asking customers too often about their attitude towards the company and its products or services can irritate the customer and create negative attitudes—the very thing the process is attempting to avoid. If the customer attitude index is slowing or turning negative, the company is in the process of moving away from alignment.

The fourth element of the balanced scorecard, and *the only leading indicator*, is employee morale. The positive morale of a group is a powerful energy source. If morale is good, it can energize the entire organization and manifest itself in positive customer interaction. If morale is low, it can, like a cancer, suck the energy out of the strongest members of the organization. In very close competitive struggles among equals, positive morale is often the deciding factor between success and failure.

Andrew Corporation, a telecommunications equipment manufacturing company in a suburb of Chicago, implemented an "empowerment" program in an effort to elevate the morale and productivity of the entire work force. Within one year, confusion and chaos reigned. After productivity dropped by 30 percent, and morale crashed, upper management pulled the plug and killed the program.

The problem, however, was not in the empowerment. The employees were more than willing to shoulder full responsibility for the outcome, and during their pre-empowerment training sessions, morale was extremely high.

Unfortunately, because middle management never understood the concept of empowerment, the employees were never given the goals and objectives of the empowerment. As a result, the mission was ambiguous, and the leadership unfocused.

As we discussed earlier, most of the resources within a company are expended at the Systems level, which consists of people, processes, and technology. The components of the Systems come together to support, produce, and deliver the company's products or services to the customer.

While the quality of the processes determines the effectiveness of the systems and the quality of the technology determines its efficiency, the people determine the responsiveness of the systems. Employees with high morale and positive attitudes are more responsive than those with low morale and negative attitudes. If employee morale is improving, you are moving towards better alignment, and if employee morale is deteriorating, you are headed for misalignment.

Employee morale will normally elude the impersonal nature of surveys and extends beyond the grasp of simple statistics. And yet it is the best indicator of the company's alignment and whether the company is moving towards or away from alignment. Since morale is vital to the organization's future well-being, how does the company measure it and, then, having measured it, how does the company improve it?

In our experience, morale can only be measured through one-on-one interviews. Employees' morale is a direct reflection of their sense of worth and respect and their optimism for their near-term future. Confidence and integrity feed this. Confidence reflects the employees' belief in their own competence, and integrity reflects their trust in the organization.

Therefore, by elevating competence and trust, the organization elevates confidence and integrity, which elevates optimism, and that, in turn, elevates morale.

Because only 5% of the employees who take an anonymous survey believe that it is truly anonymous, surveys are, at best, unreliable and, at worst, misleading. Carefully orchestrated one-on-one interviews, where an environment of political neutrality and social contribution can be established, will produce information with greater depth and applicability than will surveys.

Once we have measured morale, how do we improve it? First, leadership must understand and accept that everyone in the organization is important to the success of the organization and, therefore, deserves equal respect and trust.

The leaders are not better, nor more important, than the managers. The managers are not better, nor more important, than the workers. All have different jobs requiring different levels of skill, capabilities, knowledge, and experience. Leadership's job is to keep the company focused on accomplishing the Mission, ensuring that the Mission is the right Mission. Management's job is to eliminate the barriers to accomplishing the Mission, implementing the Strategies, and providing the Structure. The worker's job is to "responsively" fulfill the Mission, using processes designed to optimize effectiveness and technology fitted to optimize efficiency.

In order to do this, the worker must be treated fairly and with respect, and he/she must know, understand, and embrace the Mission and Strategies of the organization. Armed with the prioritized values that arise from consistent, aligned Missions and Strategies, they then can be empowered to do their jobs.

Employees in such an organization will have high morale and positive attitudes, and they will be highly responsive to the Mission and to the needs of the customer.

There are very good consulting firms who specialize in working with companies to develop and implement balanced scorecards to meet that company's specific needs. However, this should not be used as eyewash. The balanced scorecard should be implemented only after the company has made substantial progress towards aligning itself and its Directives. Otherwise, the baseline that the company establishes in its metrics will be too low.

Part II

Embracing the MBA Quest

Leading: Three Vital Processes

4

Great leaders run great companies. Great companies reflect great leaders. These stars in organizational illumination and performance achieve their goals through great *vision*, great *focus*, and great *execution*. Great focus embodies great vision, great execution embodies both. Execution materializes for the organization and its customers the exceptional mindset and balanced viewpoints of this noble class.

Many management books and other publications expound on the pivotal role the leader plays in the company's success. Targeted at those who aspire to be leaders, these books describe the characteristic attitudes, behavior and results that define the ethos of these *stars*. Provocative and eloquent, their messages stir the passions of the desirous. They lay out the footsteps for the courageous; and mark the graves of those who fell in pursuit—usually with this epitaph: "How you achieve your mission is no less important than your mission."

We concur! Vision is not timeless. Viewpoints lose their relevance. Capabilities must be renewed. If not, then the organization executes against predisposed conclusions drawn from outdated frames of reference. "That's the way we do things here."

Predisposed conclusions make for strong delusions—like pursuing the right mission in the wrong way—because the conclusions are in fact true! What? What did you say? *Listen*, what we are saying is they are true (relevant) within the context of a particular mindset. The problem is when that frame of reference is no longer timely, it becomes passé and its leaders either don't know it or are loath to admit it. It is based on another economic era or cycle.

Horses and ploughs were a productive means to the harvest in the agricultural era. The tractor changed that at the dawn of the industrial era. The transistor, computer, software, and especially web based applications and services are changing it again, but at a pace many agricultural and industrial leaders couldn't imagine; and it is accelerating with each new software release!

Our takeaway: you have to use digital means to compete in this digital age; or, re-stated as a tenet: you have to adopt the light giving mindset and its inspired perspectives as illuminated by the technological advances of that era: be it fertilizer, the combustible engine, or the transistor. Why? Because they become the impetus for new needs and better ways to serve both consumer and commercial customers. The need today and tomorrow is to do and achieve more with fewer resources (time, cost, labor, material, space, and distance) at a higher rate of quality and faster rate of return than ever before! That's the universal business need that every economic era has satisfied better than its predecessor.

The agricultural mindset became outdated and its views on productivity lost their relevance with the arrival of the industrial age. Just compare the farmer's execution with the horse and plough with the farmer's execution with the tractor. The industrial farmer saw that times had changed, the tractor was relevant, and his enterprise needed it. Viewpoints draw their perspectives from mindsets—the mental lens or frames of reference—that determine vision and focus. Beware of predisposed conclusions espoused by great leaders of another era. Great leaders of different eras share common attributes of success in terms of experience, skills, strategy, wisdom, and even values. Those don't change. They endure from one era to the next.

What does change is that a scientific and/or philosophical discovery illuminates the mind to see inventions and truths that free us from past limitations—to achieve what our forefathers thought impossible. Just consider how much faster we go and how much farther we've come with each advance in transportation power: from the horse to the automobile to the airplane to the space shuttle! From the rise of the Roman Empire to the introduction of the automobile, it required roughly two thousands years to achieve. Yet within the space of 100 years we've come from the horse and buggy age to the astronaut age. How exciting! And, yet how daunting to those *stars* that rose to their present apogee only to realize it is harder than ever to stay aligned.

Customer needs are creating both new opportunities and new threats at an accelerating pace on a global scale. No! Check that: *it's on a galactic scale*. To the scientist, their sights are set on being the first to establish a colony on another planet. To the religionist, their sights are set on breaking into a heavenly dimension where they travel like a thought and escape the limitations of time and age.

Far-fetched? To one person, yes! To another person, no! This dichotomy in perspective is what distinguishes *all-stars from stars; and, why some stars become fallen stars*. All-Stars maintain an open frame of mind. They transcend eras! They have a mind for all seasons. Stars, in contrast, are great leaders that shine within an economic dispensation. They stay aligned with customer needs within the pace of that timeframe; provided pride and prejudice don't dim their discernment.

All-Stars not only keep the noble ethos that defined success in the former time, but also remain open to the illumination of the dawning era! For this reason, their frame of reference is continually adapting with renewed possibilities that inspire them to consider either new or better ways to serve their customers. That inspiration is channeled into research, compared with customer intelligence and introspective discussions; all to validate assumptions, confirm facts, assess risk, and ultimately re-align themselves to where they see the customer going.

All-Stars never stop learning! They are active listeners. They guard against pride and prejudice. They practice active learning. Erudition preserves their brilliance. They don't fear innovation, they embrace it. Their mindset is forever young. Their views are timely; and their execution the hallmark of both. Great speed, cost structures, quality, customer relationships, financial results, market acceptance, and ultimately market valuation characterize all-star performance and it concomitant rewards.

All-Stars bridge eras. Empowered by what we describe as a three dimensional frame of reference—it equips them to see things which are, were, and will be in a unified context as they stand in the gap between the past and future missions. They announce simultaneously the setting and the rising of the sun. Through them, their present organization with its accrued reputation is able to embrace the new mindset to see the renewed means to achieve what previously was thought impossible.

These all-stars, or MBA Leaders (all-star mindset) for that is the type of mindset our framework nurtures, do not lead for the mere sake of nobility. They lead to make their constituents noble. Their constituents are their legacy. MBA Leaders can only shine through an MBA Company. Like electricity—which has the power to illuminate a room, a house, or a city; but only if its connected to a light bulb—an MBA Leader cannot fulfill his or her MBA Quest without the filament of an MBA Company. The mission requires both. The leader is the dynamics (energizer). The company is the mechanics (lamp). And the light is the fulfillment of their first purpose: to meet the recognized customer need.

The MBA Business and Strategy Leadership System

What sets the MBA Business and Strategy Leadership System (Figure 4.1) apart from its forerunners is that it develops within one holistic framework both the dynamics of an MBA Leader and the mechanics of an MBA Company. Its unique three dimensional (3D) strategy process enables both. But that's not all. That same 3D process engenders one strategic focus that melds the vertical alignment of the strategy (The MBA Quest or The What) with the horizontal alignment of the strategy (the Execution Capabilities or The How).

Figure 4.1 pictures the model as a value chain. We converted the MBA Principles Framework into the MBA Value Chain Framework for a number of reasons.

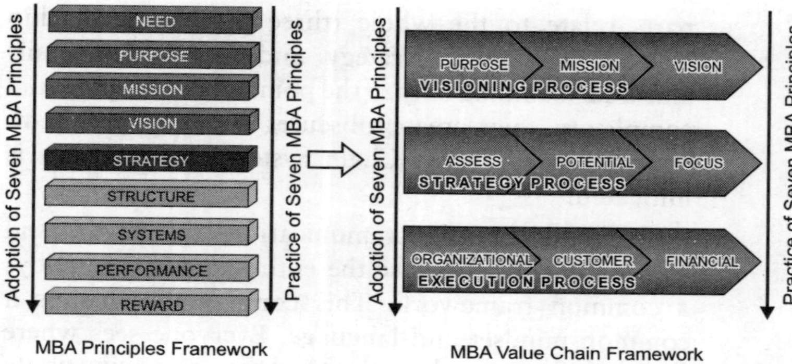

Figure 4.1: Converting the MBA Principles Framework into an MBA Value Chain Framework

1. A value chain enables process mapping. Process views show vital cause and effect relationships. Because a chain is only as strong as its weakest link, process mapping makes it easier to pinpoint weak or missing links, especially, the execution links where traction is gained or lost towards the MBA Quest.
2. It helps visualize and, thereby, enrich your understanding of the two alignments that must be integrated within one strategic focus to see the right mission and means to achieve it. The visioning, strategy, and execution processes comprise the vertical value chain alignment—which aligns the company to the long-term direction or MBA Quest. The organizational, customer, and financial perspectives constitute the horizontal value chain—which aligns the value creating linkages through time-phased investments and actions to achieve the MBA Quest. As we will come to appreciate later, "strategic themes" or the objectives of the strategy translate the long-term direction into specific process steps.
3. You can map the cause and effect relationships between them and within them (the vertical and horizontal chains) to whatever level of detail understanding dictates. And that can be done without anyone in the organization losing sight of the big picture and how the

parts relate to the whole (three primary leadership processes: visioning, strategy, and execution). Details aide understanding only to the point where the potential complexity they create obscures its original intent. With the MBA Value Chain System that tendency is mitigated.

4. It facilitates better communication up, down, and across the chain because the entire company employs a common framework. This commonality fosters a common mindset and language. Everyone sees where their link fits in and how they and their team contribute to the mission. It connects the "*we*" (functional, cross-functional, or global team) and "*I*" (individual contributor) together.
5. Value mapping removes the theoretical limitations that constrain most business and strategy leadership systems. No need to feel unique and isolated from its application due to the idiosyncrasies of your business. We are able to map client situations to the model regardless of company size or industry. The three value chain processes are present in every business, *whether they practice them or not.*

In Figure 4.1, notice that the models have two guide rails to depict the desired alignment. The left rail is labeled *Adoption of the Seven MBA Principles* while the right rail is labeled *Practice of the Seven MBA Principles*. In the value chain version, the process arrows are pointing right to show that through these processes executive leaders transform over time the principles into best practices.

Strategy as it appears in the MBA Principles Framework denotes a plan to accomplish the mission. Strategy Process, in comparison, is better because it sets forth the three steps that the executive leaders and their management teams go through to craft an unbiased strategy. As we will see in the next chapter, these three steps nurture the MBA Leadership mindset that guards against predisposed conclusions. Recall that although *they* can be true, *they* make for strong strategic delusion when based on an outdated frame of reference!

Where Structure, Systems, Performance, and Reward Fit

Figure 4.2 completes the model conversion. It shows where structure, systems, performance, and reward fit within the execution process. We see further that the Organizational Perspective focuses on value creation through its structure and systems. This perspective derives its focus vertically from the strategy process and horizontally through its alignment with the Customer Perspective. The Customer Perspective defines the customer value proposition (CVP). The CVP is really the long-term mission in operational form. The organization creates the value in accordance with its internal performance metrics to deliver against the performance expectations of the customer value proposition. We will expound more on the performance goals in chapter 6. For the present, recognize that value captured equals value delivered (price and terms) minus value created (COGS and SG&A).

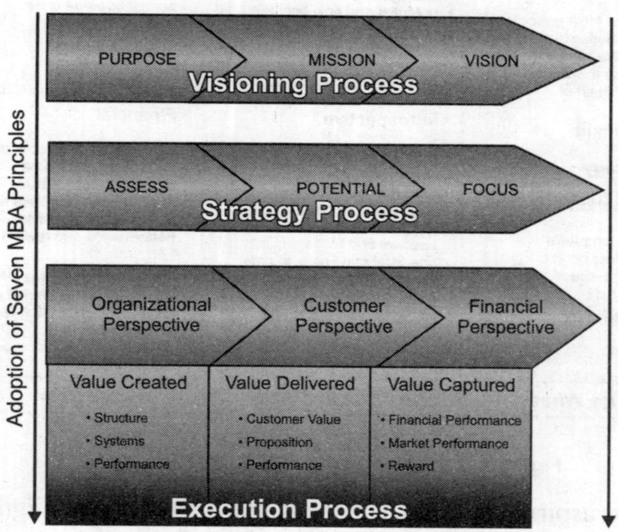

Figure 4.2: Where Structure, Systems, Performance, and Reward Fit within the Execution Process

Reward is directly proportional to how much value was captured in both quantitative (monetary) and qualitative (moral and best practices) terms. As we postulated in part one of this work, the Financial Perspective validates that profit and shareholder value are not the purpose of the company. Rather, they are lagging indicators of how well we fulfilled the recognized customer need as measured by the delta between value delivered and value created!

A Better Way to See and Energize Business Performance

Figure 4.3 presents the MBA Business and Strategy Leadership model in a form that underscores the merit of our approach: *a better way to see and energize business performance.*

A Business and Strategy Leadership System that enables...

a better way

1.0 The MBA Leadership Approach

- employs the MBA model holistically to convert MBA principles into practice in order to align the company through the vertical value chain of
- **Visioning**
- **Strategy**
- **Execution**
- to the long-term customer centric mission–***the MBA Quest.***

The What

to see and energize

2.0 The MBA Strategy Process

- is that part of the model that MBA Leaders and Managers use to see potential and how best to achieve it through three dimensions of sight:
- **Retrospective**
- **Introspective**
- **Prospective**
- Through this 3D lens–the three steps of the strategy process mind melds the Leaders and Managers into one Strategic Focus in order to cascade the vertical alignment into the horizontal alignment to achieve ***the MBA Quest.***

The What and How

business performance

3.0 The MBA Execution Process

- is that part of the model that MBA Managers use to align the three perspectives of the horizontal value chain:
- **Organizational**
- **Customer**
- **Financial**
- with the strategic focus in order to connect time phased investments to specific execution links and measure their resultant performance and reward
- The execution links are where traction is gained or lost towards ***the MBA Quest*** and validates the proverb: a *chain is only as strong as its weakest link.*

The How

Figure 4.3: Embracing the MBA Quest Framework

The aspiring MBA Leader elucidates his or her alignment role within the synchronized context of the three strategic processes: visioning, strategizing, and executing. No matter that MBA Managers within the Organizational Perspective own the actual value creation and its performance. It is through these three processes that MBA Leaders design, build, and direct an

MBA Company. At the end of the day, they are accountable for achieving the MBA Quest.

It is the Leader's job to influence the strategic job profiles of their MBA Managers. It is the Leader's job to energize the structures and systems through the MBA Managers. Therefore, the mindset of the MBA Managers and its respective viewpoints must be developed and renewed within the same strategy process that the MBA Leaders use. Otherwise, alignment between the vertical MBA Leadership processes and the horizontal MBA Management execution linkages will suffer. Vertical alignment reflects itself as the degree of accord between the leaders and managers as a product of the strategy process. Horizontal alignment reflects the degree to which the accord was implemented across the execution linkages. The MBA Strategy Process by its 3D steps forges this accord. And it does it with a mechanism (introspective step) of checks and balances to guard against pride and prejudice, the avowed enemies of sound vision, sound judgment and sound results.

Strategizing: Three Pivotal Views

5

Pivotal times require pivotal views. Pivotal views reflect pivotal minds—*all star leaders* who stand in the gap between eras, cycles, restructurings, turnarounds, and whatever momentous circumstance that drives misalignment. Energized by a three dimensional frame of reference—*they see things others cannot.* Standing alone at the junction of time, they speak of future possibilities—a vision of value—a breakthrough in value delivery and capture. For the stars and those just reaching their long sought apogee, the value gap (between where they see themselves today and where the all-star sees them in the future) is either far-fetched, daunting at best or to those whose trust is absolute—respected as thinking outside the box.

In Figure 5.1, our 2.0 MBA Strategy Process nurtures the all-star mindset that unleashes the potential for all-star performance in the process of creating its strategy.

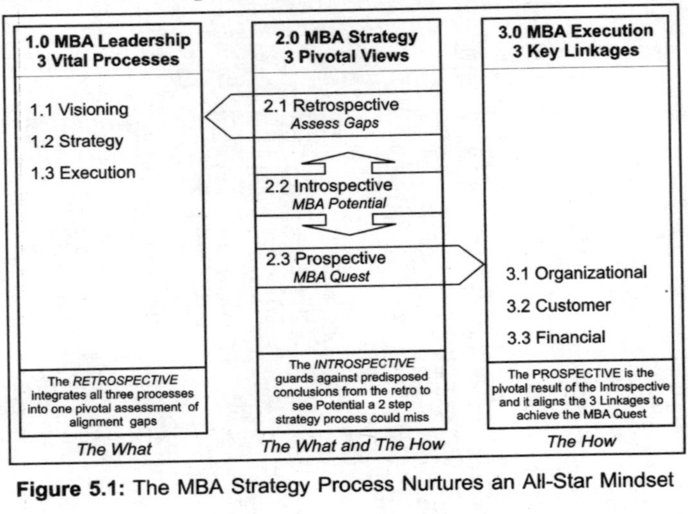

Figure 5.1: The MBA Strategy Process Nurtures an All-Star Mindset

2.1 The retrospective integrates all three executive leadership owned processes into one assessment—pivotal because it proposes scenarios of *vertical alignment* (long-term vision, strategic focus, and execution perspectives) conjointly with horizontal alignment (organizational perspective, customer perspective, and financial perspective) based on the gaps of both.

2.2 The introspective step considers the retrospective assessment with an attitude guarded against predisposed conclusions. It checks for degrees of bias, presumption, veracity, and passion. It manifests convergence between executive leaders and their management teams in the form of "*The What and The How*".

2.3 The prospective, using the output of the introspective, first locks in the vertical alignment of the leadership strategy. Next, it locks in the guiding perspectives for the management strategy. The management strategy converts the leadership strategy (strategic themes) into execution investments (action plans) whose overarching goal is to optimize value across the chain.

These three pivotal viewpoints work together like a pair of 3D glasses to help its leaders and managers see what a two-step or 2D process could miss. Recognizing this concept might seem abstract; we present the *Crossroads Allegory* to elucidate our declaration: *pivotal times require pivotal views!*

THE CROSSROADS ALLEGORY

Leading and lagging indicators: morale, time to market, cost to serve, quality, market share, company image, and financial performance are trending in the wrong direction. The Board of Directors, alarmed at what appears as a sudden reversal of events, agrees that a pivotal time has arrived and a pivotal view is vital. Accordingly, they secretly commission an all-star and a star to assess the situation in the unified context of past, present, and future performance. Their objective is to individually present a credible, yet breakthrough crossroads strategy. They are instructed to visit (at separate times) a certain *3D Cinema*. This particular *3D Cinema* was chosen because its plot, leading characters, setting, pace, and melodramatic theatrics epitomizes the challenge facing its firm.

The day of reckoning had arrived. With all directors present, the board room was bursting with anticipation and nervous energy. The star presented his findings first and the all-star proceeded second. Both strategies were methodical, appeared imaginative, and vigorously, if not eloquently, presented. After a period of question and answers, and a brief recess for the board to caucus among themselves, they met with the two stars to share their perspective on the strategic proposals.

Unanimous in their verdict, with one lone exception, they announced that the star's strategy, although daunting, was feasible and motivating. On the other hand, they viewed the all-star's strategy as far-fetched, incredulous, and quite frankly de-motivating. They felt the organization, though in need of a pivotal strategy, would not buy into the vision and, therefore, could not risk a further blow to its morale. The lone director, who abstained from the majority opinion, stated she did so because although it might be difficult to see what the all-star saw at the 3D Cinema, her esteem for the track record of this leader precluded her from doubting his credibility.

A year later, the same board met to review and discuss the results of implementing the star's strategy. Unfortunately, morale and execution were still receding. Moreover, it was now apparent that given more time, the strategy could not deliver against expectations. This prompted them to step-back and sincerely seek to understand what happened. Their sense of urgency motivated them to hire a highly regarded third party to help shed some light on the matter.

Here is what former Admiral Grace Hooper reported. Unknown to either the board or the all-star, the star viewed the cinema through 2D glasses. The glasses in form and fit were exactly like the 3D glasses, except they had 2D lens. Evidently, the cinema had agreed to cooperate with research by the local university. A team of graduate students were studying by observation the differences in physical, emotional, and verbal responses to the stimuli of the cinema when viewed with 3D versus 2D glasses. They hypothesized that on a scale of 1-10, with 10 being the strongest, the 3D viewers would evoke an average response of 8, while the 2D viewers would score an average of 3. They reasoned that the 3D response would be significantly stronger because they could see what the 2D respondent could not.

That was the first part of the study. The second part of the study called for them to interview a sample from both viewpoints to ascertain to what degree the different sensory experiences impacted what they could envisage. They found that the 3D sample group's mental images were more futuristic, yet consistent with the 3D story line, when compared with the 2D group. They concluded that a 3D sensory experience produced superior vision and judgment than the 2D perspective. They postulated that a 3D person was more likely to see more potential and the means to achieve it than a 2D person. Their challenge, however, was how to convince a 2D mindset to accept a 3D vision. Compounding the challenge is the fact the 2D's prospective is true, but less relevant because it drew upon a limited frame of reference.

The board remained silent for what seemed like forever. Finally, last year's lone abstainer stood up and broke the silence with an epigram. So, Admiral, what I hear you saying is that this board needs to have its eyes examined! We could not see the merit of our all-star's strategy because of our 2D frame of reference! Is that your message?

Admiral Hooper's first name, Grace, did not betray her sensibilities and manner. Calm, yet steadfast, she answered, "Ladies and Gentlemen, to be blind and to not know that you are blind has tragic consequences. Vision is not timeless. Viewpoints lose their relevance. Capabilities must be renewed. In this digital era, it's more difficult than ever to stay aligned to the future while delivering on the present. The pace is relentless. The scope is galactic. Regardless of present advantages in resources and scale, it only takes visionaries like XXXXX equipped with digital skills to challenge your apogee.

When I stood on the bridge of my ship, guiding my fleet through perilous waters, I had to look to more than human vision to lead the way. The wisdom garnered from past missions was invaluable, as was the success of recent strategies. However, my sense of vision and judgment had to factor in the capabilities built into my fleet (processes, people skills, and information technology) and its part in the defense network. The electronic sensors, signals, and timely classified information coupled with the battle potential of my digital weaponry, all of that together coupled with my experience and knowledge shaped my mindset and its outlook.

Always cognizant that the enemies of my flag were likewise investing in technological intelligence and weaponry and were rigorously training their military in its use, *I trained my mind and attitude* to be ever vigilant to the unexpected and alert to the improbable. Consequently, my frame of reference was always thinking five to seven moves ahead of where our intelligence network reported our adversary to be.

My challenge, however, was the same one you are facing. How do I build into the strategy process a mechanism that keeps not only my frame of reference laser sharp, but also that of my leaders and managers who participate in the shaping and executing of our strategic course? *For as you have just experienced, a 2D mindset will resist the virtues of a 3D viewpoint!*

THE MBA STRATEGY PROCESS: BUILDING IN THE POWER OF SELF-AWARENESS

Mind control, as a means to an end, is not out of the question for some of the world's military commanders. For business and strategy leaders, however, that means would be unethical and met with contempt. How then do you architect a strategy process that nurtures the right mindset, without attempting to control what one thinks? Freedom of speech is really a manifestation of freedom of thought, with one caveat: what you say, how you say it, and knowing when to say it mark the skills of a respected diplomat. Admiral *Grace* in our analogy handled a very pointed question and sensitive issue with diplomacy. She accomplished it in a manner that enabled her constituents to remain open to her prescription for corrective lens.

Freedom of thought and its timely expression are part of the dynamics that the MBA Strategy Process facilitates. Through its three dimensional steps (assess, potential, and focus) it encourages the right mental attitude of its participants. The right mental attitude creates an atmosphere where the diverse mindsets and champions of the former mission feel free to think and express themselves without the constraint of fear, intimidation, or tradition. Like a dynamo, the process should generate an ambience of positive, creative energy. This empowers leaders and managers to see and express a potential that others might not see. At the same time, it acts like a pair of self-correcting lens that enables the planners to adjust their frame of reference to envisage what before was unthinkable.

Embracing this approach requires a humble frame of mind, active listening and learning—and in that order. Learning the mechanics of the model is not enough. The right mental attitude, as the guardian against predisposed conclusions, helps to energize the company with the MBA mindset.

That said, we recognize from our experience with turnarounds that the mental and emotional strain of the financial pressure acts as a strong headwind against the virtues of an open frame of mind. Its stakeholders are disillusioned, its managers plagued with inertia, and its employees operate under a cloud of de-motivating uncertainty and suspicion. Filled with self, too many parties to the emergency are guided by salvaging their own interests versus the preservation of the company. Much finger pointing and deflective attitudes hinder attempts to stabilize the situation by cutting it back to its core strengths, so like a pruned tree; it can seize the opportunity to flourish again in another season.

We mention that to counterbalance the notion that the MBA Strategy Process is filled with pleasantries, avoids conflict, and shies away from the harsh realities of weak performance. On the contrary: it promotes robust dialog. It attempts to unveil questionable motives, objectives, and practices. It exposes environments that have become closed and stagnant. It sees through strategy processes that merely go through the motions to arrive at predisposed conclusions. And it challenges leaders and managers, by virtue of its noble mindset, to set aside pride and prejudice and see themselves as others do: too filled with self; unwilling to admit mistakes and weaknesses, and an advocate of active listening and learning in word only.

Like Admiral Grace, it expounds with tact on the tragedy of being blind and not knowing it. However, its goal is not to expose the myopic or the dim sighted—the fallen stars whose own brilliance blinded them to their real purpose. Its aim is to guard against cataracts or some other leadership illness that prevents the organization from renewing its mindset—the all-star lens that empowers great vision, great focus, and great execution.

Conflict is unavoidable. The headstrong like headwinds have their seasons. Like a trans-Atlantic fight, they make the engines work harder, the trip longer, and use more fuel in the process. However, they do not prevent the fight from reaching its destination. The MBA Strategy Process accounts for that (See Figure 5.2). It doesn't avoid it. Rather it attempts to take that resistance and re-channel it into the right mental attitude.

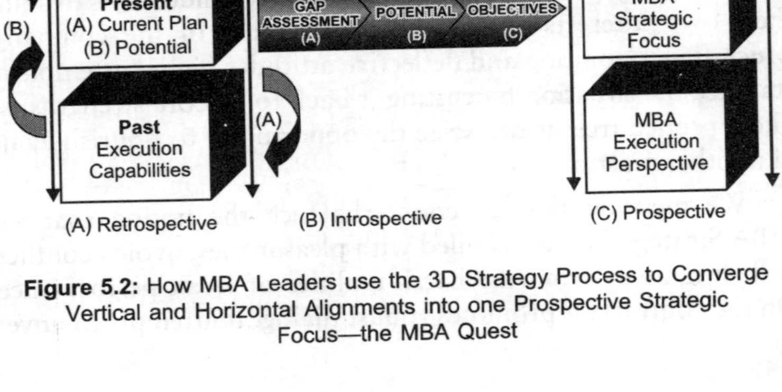

Figure 5.2: How MBA Leaders use the 3D Strategy Process to Converge Vertical and Horizontal Alignments into one Prospective Strategic Focus—the MBA Quest

In other words, the purpose of the assessment step (retrospective) is not to measure the value gap (the gap between current organizational capabilities and future possibilities) in order to find fault—and, thus, put individuals on the defensive. Its objective is to determine with the right mental attitude what should our strategy be to *close the value gap* so we can fulfill our mission—which ultimately mandates investments in process, people, technology, and the *X factor*.

The introspection step feeds off the assessment. It contemplates the right mix of corrective, preventative, and preemptive moves across credible timeframes. Its motive is not repressive, but expressive. Based on the quantitative and qualitative analysis of the retrospective, which on occasion should include third party benchmarking, its rules of engagement free all parties to the process to freely express exactly what they think with the aim of seeing and achieving the MBA potential that a 2D mindset is prone to miss.

The introspective step acts as the *self-correcting lens* for the organizational mindset. It's the step that is missing in other systematic strategy approaches. Standing in the gap between the retrospective step (the *past* in light of future possibilities) and the prospective step (the *future* strategy), it actually examines the organizational frame of mind (the collective mindset of the leaders and managers in the process) to check for bias, presumption, veracity, and passion. It's this step that makes the MBA Strategy Process 3D and empowers its proponents *to see and achieve what others cannot*.

Moving directly from the retrospective to the prospective step makes the organization vulnerable to predisposed conclusions. If the frame of reference has not kept pace with the advances of the era, then it is apt to propose a strategic focus that is relevant for that mindset, but outdated for its timeframe. That makes for a strong strategic delusion. A 2D mindset can neither envisage a 3D viewpoint nor see the folly of its own bias. In essence, the 3D strategy process builds in a step of self-awareness.

PIVOTAL TIMES DO INDEED REQUIRE PIVOTAL VIEWS

The MBA Strategy Process is the *pivotal process* of the MBA Value Chain because it equips leaders and managers with the 3D glasses or pivotal view to align their company both vertically and horizontally to the MBA Quest (See Figure 5.3). It simultaneously nurtures the dynamics of the all-star mindset (leadership competencies) and the mechanics of the all-star

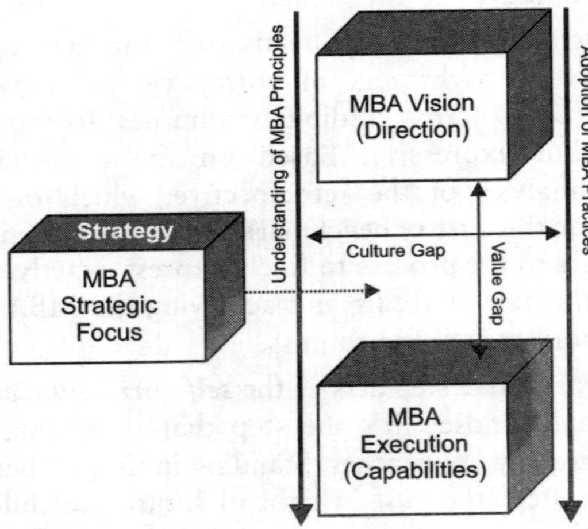

MBA Execution Capabilities represent the investments, initiatives, and metrics as driven by the Strategic Focus to bring the Capabilities in line with the Business Potential—the MBA Quest. These capabilities are best considered as a Value Chain comprised of three value optimizing Linkages.

Figure 5.3: Strategy is the *Pivotal Process* in the MBA Framework that Aligns needed MBA Execution Capabilities with the MBA Vision

company (structure and systems that drive the execution capabilities) within one balanced process. It unleashes the energy of MBA Leadership through the lamp of the MBA Company to brightly shine in the fulfillment of its purpose: to satisfy in a differentiated manner the recognized customer need.

Executing: Three Horizontal Linkages

6

Stars shine within the pace of an era, build a shared vision and point the way. Fallen stars, blinded by their own brilliance, lost sight of their purpose and the way. All-Stars, illuminated by a mind for all seasons, stand in the gap between eras, cycles, and old and new business models. They leapfrog the *shared vision approach* by building collaborative business models that cultivate a *shared mindset*. They integrate the thought leaders at all levels of the company, whether or not a manager, into the *strategy thought process* to form a constellation of lights—the MBA Mindset.

This shared mindset drives innovation not only in product and service generation, but also within all the core value creating processes: innovation management, customer management, operations management, and social and regulatory management. Descrying this pivotal point endows us with the appreciation of it strategic value. The old industrial mindset thinks of innovation narrowly within the innovation process. The mind of the digitally aware thinks of innovation synergistically across all four core processes that properly aligned drive an *innovative value creation system* (Figure 6.1).

This innovative value creation system, *think Dell*, delivers better on the customer value proposition than its competitors. As a reward it captures more financial and market value. And when shared equitably with owners, employees, and the community renews its energy to continuously improve its business model or value optimizing potential.

BEYOND A SHARED VISION

The Board in the Crossroads Allegory experienced how difficult it was to see a 3D vision with a 2D mindset. The

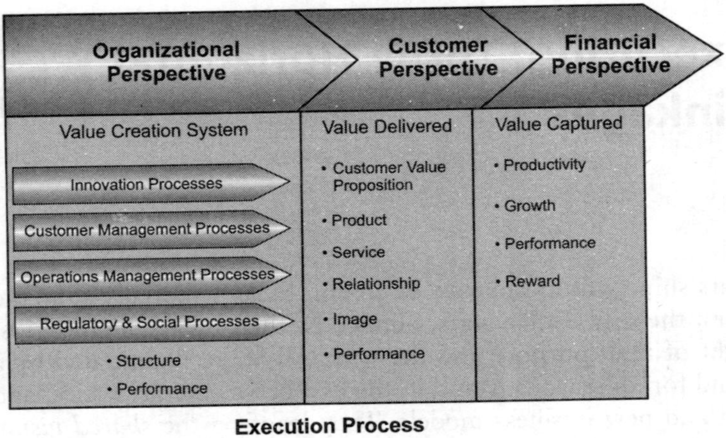

Figure 6.1: The Organizational Drivers of Value Creation Deliver on the Customer Perspective through Four Core Processes

3D glasses symbolized the all-star frame of reference that empowers a leader to envision a path between the old and new approach and to align the organization with it. This organizational alignment starts with a shared mindset. The MBA Model cultivates a shared mindset between the CEO Leadership Team, Execution Management Team, and the Non-Managerial Thought Leaders (henceforth referred to as points of light) by pulling them all—upfront—into the strategy thought process. By upfront we mean before the strategy is formulated.

This approach goes beyond a shared vision, because a shared vision should be the output of a shared mindset. In a shared mindset, the collaborative team *sees what its CEO is talking about because it's part of the corporate mind* that crafted the strategy. With the shared vision approach the CEO is *describing what he or she is looking at (thinking about)*. He or she is communicating to the execution organization after-the-fact, meaning after the strategy has already been formulated. They were not part of the strategy thought process and are now being evangelized for buy-in—that is, being asked to see what I am thinking!

Building a shared vision is a *push alignment* strategy. This approach engenders a lot of push-back because it is pushing the value creation system to execute its strategy.

Cultivating a shared mindset is a *pull alignment* strategy. It energizes a lot of pull-through because the Organizational Perspective pulls the strategic focus into itself since its own *points of light* were actively involved in its formulation. These are the program managers, project leaders, subject matter experts, and other key influencers from *all four core processes* of the value creation chain.

People support their own ideas. They are motivated to see their ideas become value added expressions. You don't have to evangelize them to believe. They become the evangelists of their own beliefs. The reality of what is possible and not possible is already factored into the strategy by the thought leaders of the execution process.

In *push* the leadership team is pushing strategic awareness down the structure into the units, functions and cross-functions responsible for its execution. It is campaigning for buy in (to another's ideas) and personal alignment by promoting a shared understanding. That takes time, lots of it, for the value creation system to comprehend and get on board.

In *pull* the strategic focus is pulled into the Organizational Perspective by its thought leaders (points of light) who were active in the thought process! They will embrace the strategy because it is expressing their mindset. They were pulled into the strategic thought process upfront. They are part of the MBA Mindset. They are part of the All-Star constellation, the alignment of thought leaders at the intersection of strategic direction (Leadership Strategy) and strategic execution (Management Strategy) (Figure 6.2). They are bought in because they were part of the collaboration process.

This makes the MBA Model both a *pull and a push* alignment model. Not everyone in the value creation system can be pulled in upfront into the strategy thought process. On the other hand, too many business models don't provide for any of this kind of collaboration; and their execution lags substantially

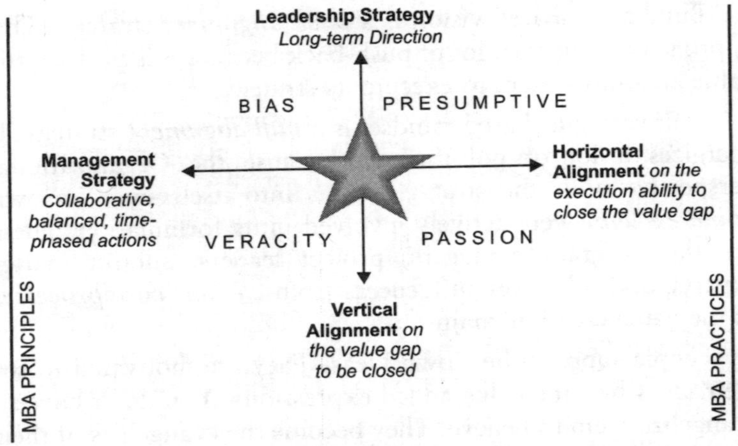

Figure 6.2: The MBA Mindset or All-Star Alignment

the announcement of the strategy. To see it (Strategic Focus) for yourself because you were part of the aligned mind that projected it versus seeking to understand what another is thinking brings the execution organization into alignment faster.

This diminishes the traditional breach between strategy formulation and execution caused in large part by the serial push approach. The MBA Model addresses that traditional weakness. Along with its other virtues, it helps CEOs close the reoccurring gap between strategy formulation and execution. It provides through its 3D strategy process a creative way to pull the points of lights into the MBA Mindset while concomitantly developing those with all-star potential into MBA Leaders.

THE MBA MINDSET: THREE STARS IN ONE

The MBA Model leapfrogs other business and strategy leadership approaches because a shared vision is the outcome of a shared mindset. Therefore, the more thought leaders at all levels of the company you can involve upfront in the mind meld, the faster your organization will become a mission-based company. The MBA Mindset (Figure 6.2) aligns the owners and executors of strategy into one constellation of lights. This all-star alignment is represented by three concentric stars at the intersection of the Leadership Strategy (long-term direction) and

Management Strategy (time phased action plans). This convergence is *the crossroads*—between leadership and management or vision of value and execution of value—that creates faster traction towards the MBA Quest.

The vertical line functions like a *plumb line*. The CEO through the three leadership processes (visioning, strategizing, and executing) plumbs the three stars to agree on the value gap. That is the gap between the long-term vision of value (MBA Quest) and your current execution capabilities. That's the Leadership Strategy.

The horizontal line acts like a *mason's level*. It horizontally aligns the three value chain perspectives on the execution capabilities needed and commitments required to close the value gap. That's the Management Strategy which is the Leadership Strategy in execution form—broken down into a step series of collaborative, balanced, and time phased action plans.

The Leadership Strategy is accomplished by the Management Strategy in a series of steps comprising vertical and horizontal planes. As Figure 6.3 depicts, a step has two faces: vertical and horizontal. The vertical face provides the direction (value vision) and the horizontal face the movement (value creation).

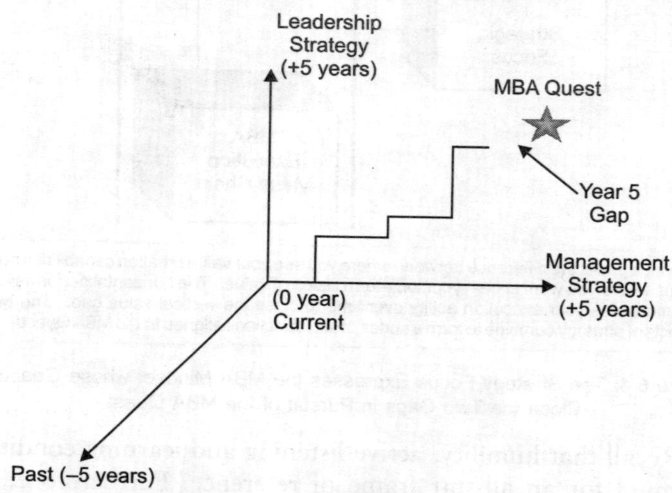

Figure 6.3: The Vertical and Horizontal Aspects of Strategy Create a Series of Step Functions (Action Plans)

The length of the value creation line or horizontal plane depicts the amount of time and investment in the execution capabilities it will take to reach the next vertical face and step up the level of performance. The gap between the top of the step and the MBA quest denotes a performance gap caused by a deficiency in the value creating assets. This performance gap can be traced to asset gaps in the Management Strategy which really measures the strategy's effectiveness. The performance gap could also be traced back to an over aggressive stretch goal in the form of the vision of value; or, it could be a combination of both: too far, too fast.

Referring back to Figure 6.2 and comparing it to Figure 6.4, you should notice they are identical in concept, except Figure 6.2 infuses the check and balance system.

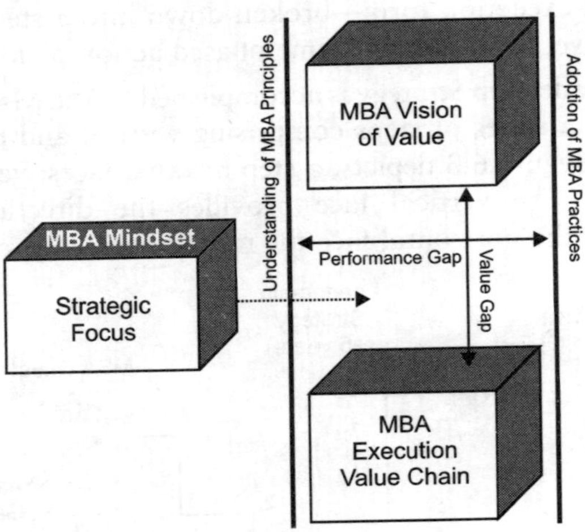

The value gap is the difference between where you see your value creation capabilities now versus where you want to be—your long-term vision of value. The horizontal performance gap measures your execution ability over time to close the vertical value gap. The two aspects of strategy combine to form a series of step functions aligned to the MBA Quest.

Figure 6.4: The Strategy Focus Expresses the MBA Mindset whose Goal is to Close the Two Gaps in Pursuit of the MBA Quest

Recall that humility, active listening and learning condition the mind for an all-star frame of reference. Furthermore, the 3D strategy process through the *introspective step* builds in a check and balance system that guards against predisposed conclusions—attributes of a static mind. The step checks for bias, presumption, veracity, and passion to ensure the potential strategy is balanced and timely in its objectives. It also is the step where we test for the degree of collaboration among the constellation star (three stars aligned in one).

Combining the all-star constellation concept together with the check and balance system enables us to create a management tool to check the qualitative alignment and balance of the strategy. To quantitatively measure the quality of strategy, we have adapted *The Balanced Scorecard*. We will tie that in later in this chapter.

Figure 6.4 appeared in chapter 5 as Figure 5.3. In Figure 6.4, the *culture* gap has been relabeled *performance* gap. Culture gap introduced the need for the aspiring MBA Company to convert over time the MBA principles into practice as a condition of executing its vision of value. That is still relevant. However, performance gap accounts for all the *asset gaps* in the value creation system that can contribute to the performance gap—remembering that the performance gap is a gap in your ability to execute the Leadership Strategy. Gap generically denotes any deficiency in the value creation system, whether it is an asset, process, or erroneous objective. It could take the form of a missing link, weak link, inconsistency, redundancy, duplication of effort or an overall *ad hoc* state with a fire fighting climate.

EPOCH CHANGE: THE STRATEGIC IMPACT ON VALUE CREATION

CEO leadership through its three vertical processes architects a firm's business model and value creation system (Figure 6.5). Strategy builds and executes the value creation capabilities across three horizontal perspectives: Organizational, Customer, and Financial. The Organizational Perspective consists of the value creation system, which in the Digital Era primarily consists of intangible assets. The Customer Perspective represents the customer view of desired value in the form of the customer value proposition for each target market. The customer value proposition is the firm's interpretation of the customer's view. The Financial Perspective is that part of the strategy that sets and measures financial expectations for how effective and efficient the value creation system delivers against customer expectations. Thus, the Financial Perspective captures the difference between value delivered (Revenue) and created (COGS and SG&A) in financial and market terms. These are represented as productivity and growth targets.

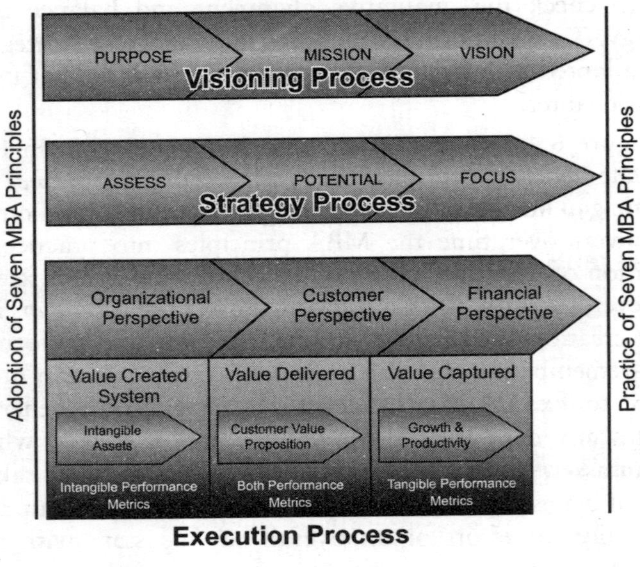

Figure 6.5: Intangible versus Tangible Assets are Driving the Value Creation System in the Digital Economy

Those are lagging indicators. They tell us how well we have done (relative to our mission), not how well we are doing. Granted, there is a correlation between the two when what you have done is still timely and within the three to five-year plans. That said, most three to five-year plans don't accurately predict economic cycles—the pivot point where the economy expands and contracts—and they find themselves with too much or too little capacity. Notwithstanding the negative financial impact, the former is far more damaging than the latter in terms of company climate, image, customer and partner relationships, and employee morale. All the attributes relevant to the health of the firm's intangible value creation system!

But the Financial Perspective doesn't capture that view of the execution process. Those are intangibles, unseen to the industrial mindset. Yet they help us measure how well we are doing now, our firm's mindset—positive or negative—and most importantly our capacity to change. Our ability to adapt to the pivot points, whether down, flat, or up. Because the financial forecast, which drives strategy and budgets in the industrial era, is a projection of historical trends, it tends to set growth goals too high and, thus build in more capacity than needed. Hence, the move to outsourcing, off-shoring, and the growth in agencies contracting with knowledge workers to augment the capacity needs of firms that are becoming more service versus product-driven. This trend is not only for lower costs and improved gross margins, it is also to offset the risk inherent in missing the pivot points—which the industrial mindset with its financially driven focus is prone to repeatedly miss.

The industrial mindset and its financial approach to strategy has been shaped through years of focus on a value creation system comprised mainly of tangible assets (plant, equipment, inventory, and cash flow) whose inputs and outputs are physical product. This has developed into an unconscious management style we characterize as *out of sight-out of mind*. It also helps to explain that since the raising of the internet flag which marked the pivot point between the industrial and digital economic eras, the gap between strategy formulation and execution is widening!

The digital economy is managed with the internet eye, and not merely the human eye. *The human eye uses the digital eye to see* customer needs and build the new kind of value creation system to service them. This digital perception is heavenly in scope: GPS, satellites and space stations. It has the power to communicate and service millions of customers at once, and the intelligence to understand better than before things which *are, were, and are to be*. It doesn't rely merely on the financial perspective to drive and measure strategy; it aligns the intelligence of all three perspectives in a value stream characterized by an intangible asset base (X-factor, people, technology, and process) that can be greater than 75% of the capital structure.

The industrial mind stands in awe of the potential. Unfortunately, it is intimidated by the scope and pace of change; and is content to ride its legacy into retirement. It is focused on a value creation system that is tangible in composition and output and driven by a financially oriented strategy. The digital mind is focused by means of digital networking on a value creation system that is intangible in composition and output and driven by a MBA Quest—a customer centric strategy!

That makes all-stars digitally minded! It's their chief listening post; delivers real time learning information when, where, and how they want; and enables them to see the zone of opportunity in a way other's can't. What is *out of sight-out of mind* for the industrial era star is ***insight-in mind*** of the digital all-star.

Humbled by continuous success, always listening, always learning, these shining examples of a mind for all seasons reflect their virtue through a 3D strategy process whose strategic focus builds an intangible value creation system aligned to the customer perspective and whose performance is continually monitored by the intelligence built into all three perspectives.

As we are about to explore, the Organizational Perspective employs intangible metrics to set and monitor performance relative to plan. The Customer Perspective does the same thing using a combination of tangible and intangible metrics—the end purpose to monitor whether or not our interpretation and articulation of the customer value proposition is in the same line of sight as the customer's. Consequently, the execution process of the MBA Model monitors its performance digitally through leading and lagging indicators—a balanced point of view.

THE FORCES OF EPOCH CHANGE

The strategic impact of this epoch shift is that the mindset, business model, strategy approach, and performance management system are being forced to change. Those who *resist* will survive for a season. Those who *comply* can have their shining moments. However, the constant pressure of managing out of sight-out of mind burns out these aspiring stars. Those who *commit* to the transformational change through a *pull model* will find the source of energy and continual innovation that is refreshing to customers, invigorating to employees and satisfying to its leaders and owners. The grid of Figure 6.6 compares and contrasts the forces of this epoch change.

Industrial Era	Digital Era
Product and Labor Driven	Service and Knowledge Driven
Tangible Value Creation System	Intangible Value Creation System
Tangible Output	Intangible Output
Tangible Metrics	Intangible Metrics
Driven by the Financial Perspective	Driven by a Balanced Perspective
Build it—Sell it Model	Sell it—Deliver it Model
Human Vision	Digital Vision
Out of Sight-Out of Mind Strategy	Insight-in Mind Strategy

Figure 6.6: The Forces of Epoch Change

MANAGEMENT STRATEGY: ENHANCING AND EXECUTING AN INTANGIBLE VALUE CREATION SYSTEM

In Figure 6.5, we saw that intangible assets within the Organizational Perspective drive its value creation system. In the next graphic, Figure 6.7, we relabeled them strategic themes. The Management Strategy breaks down the long-term Leadership Strategy into time phased action plans that both enhance and execute the intangible value creation system. This break down of the MBA Quest into a series of steps takes the form of strategic themes. These strategic themes correspond to the four core value creating processes of the Organizational Perspective. Associated with each core process are the intangible assets of people, technology, and the X-factor. Together with their respective process they form a sub-system or sub-value chain. This sub-value chain must be aligned within itself and synergistically with the other core processes to optimize its value creation.

Like the peeling back of an onion, this next section presents a series of diagrams that unfold these processes, assets, metrics

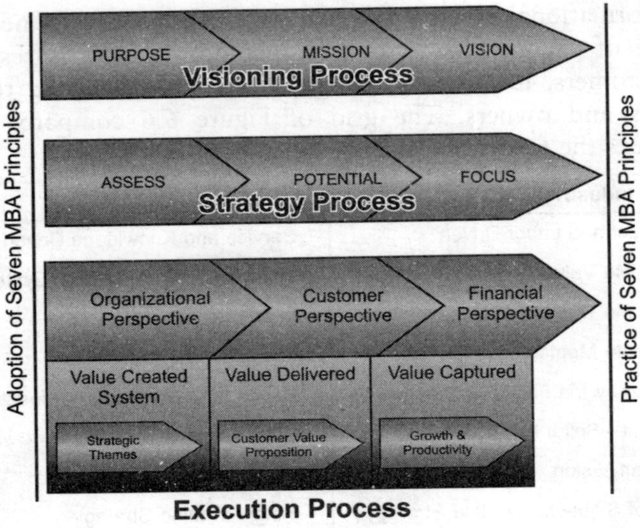

Figure 6.7: The Strategic Focus takes the MBA Quest (Vision) and Breaks it Down in the Management Strategy as Strategic Themes

and linkages. Within these levels of detail we can clearly identify and map the assets gaps as the root causes of the performance gap. Using an adaptation of the Balanced Scorecard we can also link the components and objectives of each sub-system in measurable ways for each of the strategic themes. The Balanced Scorecard and its ensuring refinements were created by Robert S. Kaplan and David P. Norton as an intangible asset alignment tool to help leaders execute strategy.

The next two figures (Figures 6.8 and 6.9), complete the top level development of the intangible value creation system. R&D, Sales and Marketing, Operations, and Regulatory and Social comprise the functional links of the Organizational Perspective. They are accountable for their respective core process as presented in Figure 6.9.

The Management Strategy will drive priorities and investments in one or more of the core processes through its break down into strategic themes. Figure 6.9 reveals the intangible assets as links in the sub-chain that together with its core process form a sub-system of value creation.

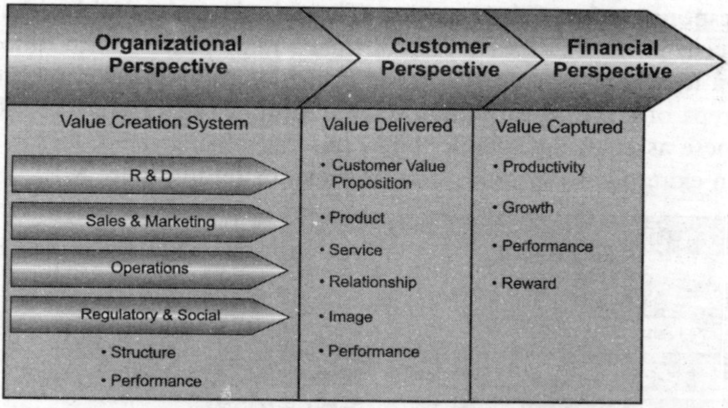

Each of these internal functions own a respective core process that via Strategic Themes direct its value chain innovation. They align synergistically to deliver on the performance expectations of the Customer Value Proposition which is the Mission in operational form.

Figure 6.8: The Organizational Functions that Own the Core Processes that Drive Value Creation Innovation

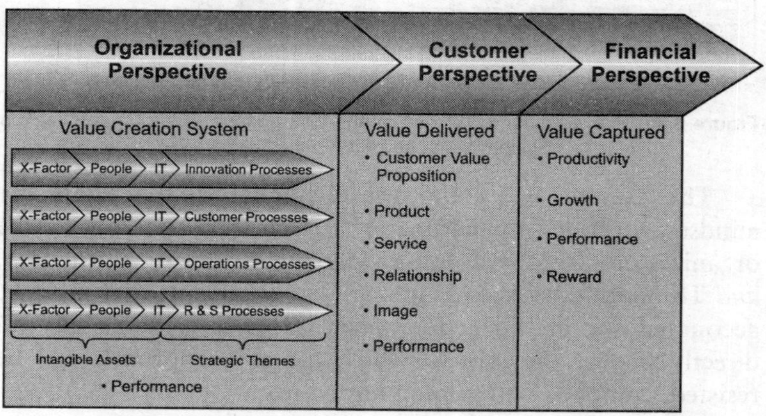

The intangible assets and their respective core process comprise each of the sub-value chains. The strategic themes not only prioritize process improvements, but also impact improvement plans for the associated intangible assets.

Figure 6.9: The Organizational Drivers of Value Creation Exploded into Four Sub-Value Chains with Assets

Each of the sub-process linkages can be further exploded into lower level maps by the functions or program teams responsible for their execution. These explosions would initially occur in the *assessment* step of the strategy process with follow on iterations as required in the *potential* and *focus* steps (three steps of strategy formulation). For simplicity, we will describe these assets using a table. First, however, using the X-factor as an example, we provide a sample explosion in Figure 6.10.

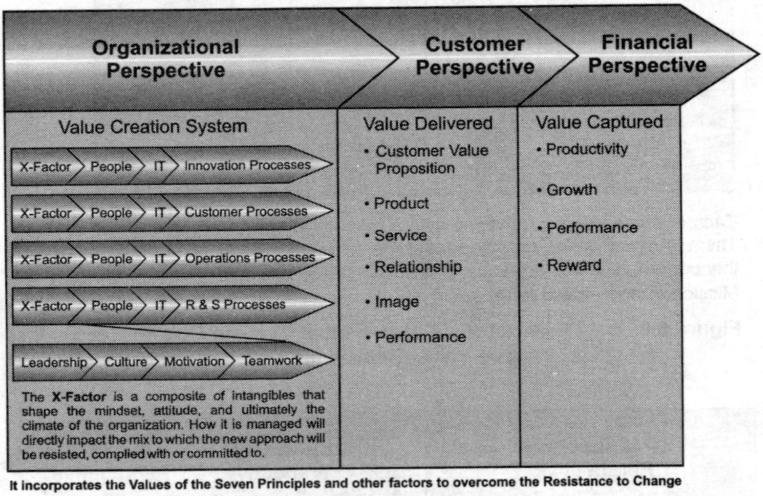

Figure 6.10: The X-Factor is Treated as the Cornerstone of the Value Creation System because of its Pull Potential

The *X-factor* is a composite of intangibles that shape the mindset, attitude, and ultimately the climate and *pull* of the organization. It consists of *Leadership, Culture, Motivation, and Teamwork*, a series of intangible investments that must be accounted for in the action plans. How it is managed will directly impact the mix to which the new approach will be resisted, complied with or committed to.

In the table entitled Sub-System Asset Gaps and Processes (Figure 6.11), we further explode the X-factor and all the other linkages in the value creation system.

The attributes of the three intangible assets (X-factor, People, and IT) are common to all four processes. That said, the actual people skills for the customer management processes will be different *vis à vis*, for example, the operations management

X-Factor	People	IT	Processes
Leadership Gaps • Leadership Model • Leadership Capacity	**People Gaps** • Strategic Job Families • Strategic Job Profiles • Training	**Application Gaps** • Transformational • Analytical • Transaction Processing	**Innovation Management** 1. Opportunity ID 2. R&D Portfolio 3. Design-Develop 4. Launch
Culture Gaps • Values • Standards • Practices		**Infrastructure Gaps** • Physical • Management	**Customer Management** 1. Select 2. Acquire 3. Retain 4. Grow
Motivation Gaps • Personal Goals & Incentives Aligned to Strategy • Reward Mix • Work Environment		**Security Gaps** • Internet • Intranet	**Operations Management** 1. Plan 2. Source 3. Make 4. Deliver 5. Returns
Teamwork Gaps • Cross-Boundary Collaboration • Best Practice Sharing • Communities of Expertise			**Regulatory & Social** 1. Management 2. Environment 3. Health/Safety 4. Employment 5. Community

Figure 6.11: Intangible Asset Gaps and Core Process Steps

processes. That same variation is applicable to the other two asset links. Although a company will have an overall culture, each unit or function within that company will have its own sub-culture, IT needs, enabling and supporting processes.

Having dissected the intangible value system, we are now ready to consider the potential range of metrics (Figure 6.12) applicable to the performance measurement of each perspective. As emphasized earlier, this is a balanced view of the strategic performance. It offers us the insight to adapt our programs, tactics, and strategic path, if necessary, in anticipation of environmental pivot points. Fully developed, it empowers the company to be more proactive to change versus reactive.

With all that in mind—the all-star mindset, its pull alignment approach, how the two gaps are closed through a series of time phased step functions, each with a vertical and horizontal strategy face, the epoch force of intangible assets on the value creation system: its composition, alignment, metrics, and customer focus, let us see how it all comes together in an adaptation of The Balanced Scorecard Plan into the MBA Model.

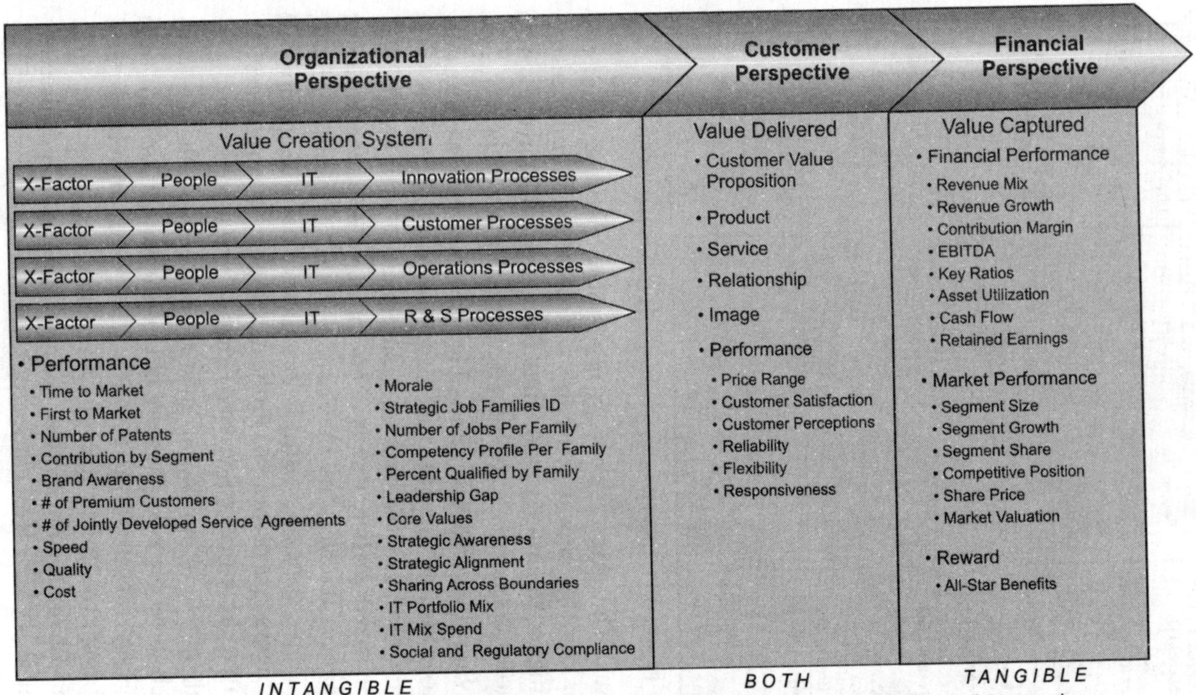

Measuring the Performance of Intangible and Tangible Assets provides visibility of Leading and Lagging Indicators and a Balanced Performance Perspective of the business.

Figure 6.12: Value Optimization Performance Measures

Figure 6.13 presents a generic template of The Balanced Scorecard Plan except for a few selections we have made to illustrate a change in vision and its strategic impact. Notice that the Organizational Perspective consists of all four links of each sub-value chain. The Customer Perspective likewise lists the objectives of its customer value proposition. And the Financial Perspective does the same.

Three sections comprise the grid. The value chain arrows depict our ability to value chain or strategy map the cause and effect relationships among the three execution perspectives. This paints a big picture visually and affords rapid creativity when used in conjunction with brainstorming, affinity diagrams, storyboards, and other relevant collaborative tools. The Balanced Scorecard section assigns measures to both intangible and tangible assets. Aligned objectively and with measures, the action plan converts the cause and effect relationship into specific steps that tie to personal and team goals. This is where traction is gained or lost towards the MBA Quest.

You will notice in each perspective we have selected by *wording and "X" marks* objectives to provide a brief example of this alignment tool's application. Let's say that based on customer trends, our vision of value calls for a change from a product-driven to a product and service-driven company. Accordingly, our strategy across the three perspectives has to change to accommodate this overarching goal. We now need a service creation system attuned to a service and relationship customer value proposition. Financially we are looking for a growth in sales and customer mix.

Given this scenario, our strategy would enumerate the strategic themes that define the nature of and priorities that will drive the innovation of core processes. Remember that there is one Balanced Scorecard Plan corresponding to one strategic theme. And that strategic theme drives one specific process improvement.

Look closely at the objectives of the Customer Perspective in Figure 6.13. Notice that customer management is the process selected. That indicates the strategic theme would be something

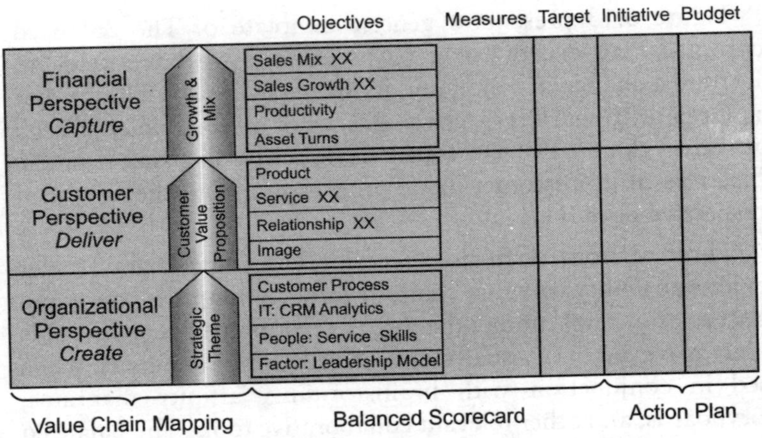

Figure 6.13: One Strategic Theme per Balanced Scorecard Plan

like this: *create a service and relationship customer management process*. This objective has a chain reaction effect on the need for CRM analytics, new job families, skill profiles, and a leadership model that cultivates executives with a service driven mindset.

Having laid down the strategic impact of epoch change on the building of the value creation system and its ensuing execution, we now return to the Crossroads Allegory to help reinforce its reality.

THE CROSSROADS ALLEGORY CONTINUED

The Chairman of the Board removed her glasses, wiped them off, and with contemplation in her voice, thanked former Admiral Hooper for her research, insights, and recommendation. She acknowledged that a 2D mindset would be challenged to see the virtues of a 3D viewpoint. She marveled at the cleverness of the university experiment, even if at her expense. Humbled by it all, she panned the faces of the Board to assess the impact of the message on their demeanor. She saw marvel, regret, determination, and relief.

To Mr. Determination she said, "Where do we go from here?" Without hesitation he replied, to the 3D Cinema! To which Miss Marvel quipped, "And let's make sure we all get

3D glasses!" Mrs. Relief, last year's lone dissident, laughingly said, "Why don't we just hold back on further expenditures, I think we have learned our lesson. "Yeah, I agree," chimed Mr. Regret. I think we should invite the all-star back, perhaps he could fit us with those self-correcting lens."

Sensing an opening, Admiral Hooper, exclaimed, "Splendid idea—there is nothing like the release of endorphins to ease the pain of reality. We may have lost a battle, but we can still win the war. To retreat to advance, in this case, is courageous. If you don't mind, I would like to be present during your laser surgery."

Composed and honored to restate his case, the All-Star framed the discussion by reviewing the objectives of the meeting:

- Revisit his alignment model
- Help them to see what they missed
- Agree on next steps

The Admiral, with the Board's permission, provided the All-Star with their curriculum vitas (resumes) and Myers Briggs types. Collectively their business mindset was shaped through numerous years of experience in the design, manufacture, and marketing of products (commercial and consumer). No one had any depth in the generation and delivery of services, except one member: Mr. Determination held the position of Senior Vice President of Customer Support; and although service oriented in principle, its focus was product support.

The All-Star began by stating that he also was unaware of the university research. He was perplexed by what he could only justify as unexplainable omissions on the part of his star colleague. Knowing now that he saw and engaged in a sensory experience much richer than his 2D associate, he felt obliged to help the Board overcome its tendency towards predisposed conclusions.

The Board sensing his empathy relaxed its guard and warmly radiated its eagerness for his retrospective. The CEO or Mr. Regret as we have come to know him, politely interrupted, to say, "Michael, to retreat to advance is noble. We welcome the opportunity to understand why our star's strategy failed and yours will succeed. Please continue."

Appreciative of their renewed confidence, he began by qualifying the CEO's statement by pointing out it has a strong propensity to succeed. As you know, *you can't put new wine in old wine skins*. Dried out, brittle and wore thin, they cannot stretch to accommodate the expansion of the still fermenting wine. Bursting open, they waste the moment to toast the accomplishment of a job well done—in good taste, with a fine sense of savor and invigorating power. Likewise in business, the creativity, energy, and vision of a new mindset cannot be poured into an old business model. Its strategy process is static. Its value creation system is inflexible and fraught with hidden gaps; and its organizational climate marked by over-commitment, fire-drills, and bouts of burnout.

Ms. Marvel, President of Keepsake Enterprises, a consumer products company, exclaimed, "Cheers, I'll toast to that. Well said. I like your point. And to that may I add...and neither can we continue to build a new service business from the old parts of our product-driven model. Patch work quilts make for great heirlooms. Building a service-driven value creation system from the relics of a product-driven one cannot consistently deliver on the new value proposition. For example, our customer support IT system is designed for a low cost model: high volume, low touch. Yet our new model is low volume, high touch: a higher margin model. No wonder our customers are complaining! They are expecting more and we are delivering less!

Glasses in place, the Chairman of the Board clearly saw the Board's mood as not so much worried about fixing blame for past missteps, but eager to find the way forward. Pleased, she was thinking that the All-Star and Ms. Marvel made a charming couple: he the prince of analogies and she the princess. Not one to wander off point, she snapped back to moment at the response of the All-Star. Your star's vision of value hit the mark, which if you recall we were aligned on that point. To remain a leader in your industry, we agreed changing customer needs dictated your attempt to reposition the company from a pure product player to a *product and service provider*.

The margins are higher and the growth prospects bright. But even more important, your commercial customers are begging for a consultative relationship to help integrate people, process, and technology in their own business to drive innovation through an increasingly intangible value creation system. Not exactly aware this is their ultimate need and the forces driving it, they do recognize the following:

- Accelerating technological convergence
- Total cost of ownership versus mere product price is a better decision criteria
- The failure in the past for some technologies to deliver as strategic investments because automation alone isn't a panacea for broken or undefined processes.

Customers no longer want to purchase products, piecemeal, department by department through an indirect channel. They are demanding more value. They want a direct service that architects an integrated solution based on their specific business needs. And that in turn demands a transformation in everything about you as company: your mindset, business model, strategy, and culture.

The vision of value is correct. The estimation of the vertical value gap was not. It was understated; and for the reason Ms. Marvel has already underscored: he (star) thought he could leverage the old value creation system more than reality would afford. That is not all, the error of the Leadership Strategy cascaded and compounded into the Management Strategy because the estimation of the horizontal gap was also smaller. Consequently, the star's strategy not only underinvested in the value creation system, but it also had the wrong priorities or strategic themes. Of course execution suffered and morale with it.

Pausing to read his audience, Mr. Determination quickly jumped in with a bit of push-back. He said, "I agree we underestimated the gaps and consequently underinvested. However, I am not convinced our priorities were amiss." Ms. Relief, his known ally, interceded. She said, "until he helps us to see what our star missed in the 3D Cinema, aren't we prone to presumption?" Mr. Regret, sensing the meeting was coming to a crescendo nodded in agreement and diplomatically took the reigns. He said, "Michael, I think we have retreated to the point we are now ready to charge forward—help us understand what we missed—what did you see that our 2D star did not?"

For the first time today, the Admiral felt anxious tension enter the room. At that queue even Michael appeared to show signs of trepidation. But recognizing his shining moment had come, he answered, "*I saw the law of inverse focus.*" And our star did not? Mr. Determination replied impulsively. He was *told* about it. He had it *described* to him in the movie. *But he never saw the law in practice*. Therefore, as evidenced by his strategic focus, he paid it no-mind. His product-driven frame of reference overrode a pivotal lesson. And I trust this Board will not, because it is difficult for a product-driven mindset to see a service focused strategy, because that focus is inversely related to its traditional way of thinking.

- The law of inverse focus states that the sales and value creation process for a service-driven business is inversely related to that of a product-driven model; and therefore its strategic focus must also be inversely related.

This has a huge impact on how the customer judges value (for products versus services) relative to the value creation process that creates it. That, in turn, is pivotal for strategy because it should be driven by how the customer evaluates our value offering. And that drives how and when we build the value creation system. For in products, the customer in most cases is indifferent to how you build the product so long as it meets expectations. The opposite is true for services. Because they are buying a promise—which doesn't exist until you deliver it, how you create it has a dramatic impact on the customer's perception of value and satisfaction. Therefore, how you order your strategic priorities or strategic themes for the service system is critical to success or failure.

For products it is a serial approach in this order:

- Innovation Management (design and develop)

- Operations Management (build)
- Customer Management (sales and delivery)

For services it is a parallel approach with a variation of order and emphasis depending on the business:

- Innovation-Customer-Operations Management (solution, sales and delivery)

Because Operations Management appears last in the parallel chain does not diminish its value—just the opposite—it is critical to ultimate success.

Serial and parallel defines your strategic themes and investment priorities. The product path is clear cut. The service road is not. It is a blend that requires the right mix and timing. If you get it wrong, as the star did, then the value creation system that the customer sees—*not the product, the system itself*—produces the wrong perceptions and leads to dissatisfaction. That is why Operations Management is crucial to the realization of customer satisfaction; it is the last thing the customer sees in the value chain.

Your star undervalued its role. This is not surprising because in a product business among the three core functions named, Operations Management relative to the other two receives the least amount of stock options. It is perceived as a COGS function, whereas R&D and Sales and Marketing are seen as keys to revenue growth. But in the service chain, Operation Management plays a leading role in revenue growth. Moreover, inversely to product operations which is characterized by tangible assets (plant, equipment, inventory, and cash flow), service operations consists primarily of intangible assets: people, process, technology, and culture. They are considered an expense in the product realm, but a strategic investment in the service realm.

These are the inverse lessons and strategic insights I came to appreciate through my 3D glasses. They changed the way I thought about services. And my strategic focus reflected it. You thought it was incredulous and de-motivating because you weren't mentally prepared for that scope of transformational change.

The Chairman of Board, spoke next. "Michael, I am starting to catch the vision. Your insights are compelling and powerful. However, you have yet to disclose what you saw that our star did not." The Board nodded in agreement. They were following him.

"I am coming to that," Michael replied. "Bear with me. I will cover the two customer scenarios where I saw the law in practice, but first allow me to share with you what we both saw. It will help to crystallize what I already said. Then I will show you a graphical depiction of my insights to help you frame a mental picture. And then we're ready to cap off this review with what I actually saw. Is that o.k.?"

Mr. Regret said, "Please proceed."

Industrial Era	Digital Era
Product and Labor Driven	Service and Knowledge Driven
Tangible Value Creation System	Intangible Value Creation System
Tangible Output	Intangible Output
Tangible Metrics	Intangible Metrics
Driven by the Financial Perspective	Driven by a Balanced Perspective
Build it—Sell it Model	Sell it—Deliver it Model
Human Vision	Digital Vision
Out of Sight-Out of Mind Strategy	Insight-in Mind Strategy

Here is a data table describing how a product and a service business are inversely related. Notice it does not state the law of inverse focus. That was my deduction and key 3D learning. The data table makes readily apparent the contrast between the tangible, visible, and five senses oriented product realm and the intangible, invisible, and perception oriented service realm. A product-driven business is a built it—sell it model whereby the customer's five senses can demo and use the product in a trial run to make a value and purchase decision. The focus is on the product. In a service-driven business the approach is just the opposite. It is a sell it—deliver it model whereby the customer's perception of value judges the credibility of the promise and the capability to deliver it. Their five senses are used to confirm their perception of value during the delivering phase. But the expectation of value which drives customer satisfaction is set by the sales process and confirmed or denied in the delivery process which is why in services the focus is on the value creation system. In services the value creation system starts with the Customer Management Process and ends with the Operations Management Process. My strategic focus reflected this knowledge.

Based on the table data and what I saw through the 3D glasses, here is a drawing I constructed to illustrate the law of inverse focus.

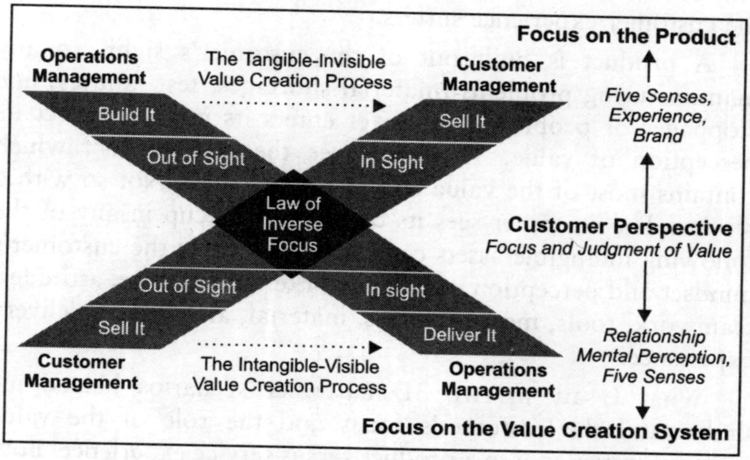

The Law of Inverse Focus Illustrated

One last subtle point and then I will speak to what I saw. Although the product model is tangible and visible centric, its value creation process in the customer's eyes is not. It is out of sight. Hence, the customer focuses on the product which contains most of the value add. Very little is left to be added through the sales process. The opposite is true in the service model. Although it is intangible and invisible centric, its value creation process is not. It is in-sight. Hence, the customer focuses on the value creation process to establish expected value which starts with the Customer Management Process (the promise) and ends with the Operations Management Process (the promise materializing).

In products how it is built is out of sight-out of mind. In services how it is delivered is in sight-in mind. Therefore, in services, the law of inverse focus states:

- How you deliver the service has to be equal to or better than how you sold it.

How you sold it creates the customer's expectation of value and how you will deliver it—their expectation of your delivery capabilities. At the very least these two value creation processes must be equal in quality of execution. If not, as the star found out, because he undervalued the Operations Management role, the customer experience suffers.

A product is built out of the customer's sight, so any manufacturing problems (material shortages, test failures, line stoppages or people issues) never enters its mind to affect its perception of value. They only see the end product which contains most of the value add in a fixed state. Not so with a service. The customer sees its delivery. A hiccup in any of the following intangible assets can negatively affect the customer's mindset and perception of value: worker appearance, attitudes, teamwork, tools, methodologies, material, and overall delivery experience.

What I saw in two 3D customer scenarios helped me understand the customer's focus and the role of the value creation system in it in a product versus service experience. Both scenarios portrayed a fine dining experience of a couple on their honeymoon. In the first scenario the meals were prepared out of sight-out of mind in the kitchen. In the second scenario the meals were prepared in sight-in mind at the dining table.

The restaurant's food and ambience was noted for five star qualities.

The food prepared in the kitchen is akin to the product built in the factory out of sight-out of mind. The customer's focus is on the product arriving and operating as expected. The food prepared at table side is akin to the service being delivered in sight-in mind on the customer's site.

In the kitchen scenario, the meals arrived, were presented, and tasted exactly as expected. Result: five star experience.

However, during the meal's preparation, the couple did not see what I saw. A member of the staff had a cold and was sneezing. The chef's apron was soiled to the point it reeked and was offensive. At the start of the meal's preparation the organic vegetables were not in stock—they arrived just in time. Finally, the couple was totally unaware of the heated exchange between the waiter and chef. But who cares, the final product arrived and tasted as expected. It had no effect on their appetite.

In second scenario the meal was prepared at table side. The quality of the food was exactly of the same high standards as the first scenario. The chef in this case had bad breath and lacked the personality to carry on an entertaining conversation with his guests. His appearance was clean but not refined. While preparing the salad, he accidentally spilled some on the table. Finally, the bowls containing the ingredients for the meal, were suitable for the kitchen, but not for presentation in front of the customer.

As expected, the couples' appetite was dampened by the manner of preparation and presentation. Their mood became somber as they begin to realize that their cherished moment was not going to live up to expectations. Although in the end the food had the same delicious potential as the other meal, they only picked at their food and left disappointed. Their experience was three stars.

Mrs. Relief was smiling to herself. The Princess of Analogies started applauding. Mr. Determination was holding out, "Michael, with all due respect, I now think I see through the lens of this law of inverse focus what you saw through your 3D glasses. However, as fond as I am of fine dining (and golf, Mr. Regret interjected, Mr. Determination smiled back for he had a tee time that very afternoon), I would appreciate an example based on our business."

The Admiral had to restrain herself. She could hardly hold her peace. At the urging of the Chairman, she and Michael had visited a customer of the new service just last week. The client was a defense contractor for the federal government.

I would be glad to do so, sir. Based on an interview with The Atomic Boat Company, here is what I found. Your sales process was perceived to be very professional. It established positive expectations for your promised solution (hardware, software, supplies, customer support, account management, and financing) and your delivery capabilities.

Unfortunately your delivery approach did not receive the same professional grade. It was judged amateur. According to the client's Senior Project Manager, she reported that during the sales pursuit you brought your "A team" and utilized an impressive technology tool called First View. First View was used by your technical consultants to assess a sample site from the client's business in order to analyze the current technical architecture and total cost of ownership. This was then used with the client's initial specifications for a Service Level Agreement to design and price a future state for that sample site—the idea being it could be extrapolated to other sites and/or units of their business to get a total solution estimate.

However, when it came to your delivery team, it was a mixture of A, B, and C players. She didn't expect the entire team to be at the senior level. However, in their attitudes, appearance, communication, and approach to the job, she expected the same professional approach that influenced her expectations—which it was not. Moreover, she found it especially troubling that First View was used to set the benchmark and sell the service, but was not used to deliver it! She said, "The current state assessment and future state design process were manual and very low tech." She found consistent errors in the report and omissions in tasks.

The Atomic Boat Company's customer story validates the law of inverse focus. From the customer's perspective, *how you deliver the service must be equal to or better than how you sold it.* Your execution is suffering because of the wrong strategic focus. Although the solution consists of technology from across your product divisions and associated partners, which is fine, the value creation system is creating expectations it cannot deliver on. You overinvested in the customer management side and underinvested in the operations management side. It is negatively affecting teamwork, motivation, and culture. The sales team is pointing the finger at the delivery team. The reality is you have a leadership gap: a star that due to the epoch forces of change has failed to internalize the law of inverse focus.

Mission-Based Alignment bridges these gaps and focuses our vision on the customer. Finger pointing vanishes because every part of the company is in alignment with the mission and the goal of understanding and meeting the Need of the Customer.

Conclusion

Economic epochs drive paradigm shifts that misalign companies. Predisposed to the mindset of the former era, top performing CEOs, Presidents and Senior Vice Presidents see market challenges and opportunities through a perspective that insists on an antiquated strategy. Result: value creation capabilities (assets) are misaligned to the demands of the new market.

The capabilities of the agricultural economy became misaligned to the preferences of the industrial era. Autos replaced horses, refrigerators cooled the demand for ice, and electricity darkened the production of kerosene lamps. Investments in plant, equipment, material, and labor sparked the need for a new system—the Du Pont financial system, as it became known, to project, track and report the performance of those tangible value creating assets.

Deja vu for the e-commerce era: the tangible value creation strategy of the industrial era lags—quickly falls behind and out of step with—the pace and diversity of demands serviced by the internet marketplace. Its value creation system is intangible (leadership, people, process, and technology) and more service versus product aligned. Consequently, the management All-Stars (Dr. Robert S. Kaplan and Dr. David P. Norton) of the new era developed a Balanced Scorecard management system to not only measure the ROI of the intangible assets, but also employ them as leading indicators of Mission-Based Alignment. That is, with one caveat: you are truly open to on-going thought leadership and the renewed strategy perspective it energizes. Then and only then can you continually align your value creation capabilities to the direction of the every changing customer need.

Granted, consumers never asked for the internet. It was scientists and academia that appreciated the value of such a fast and comprehensive research and collaboration tool. Nevertheless, once the commercial application of that communication network was made available through the world-wide-web, it opened up a vast new frontier of possibilities to satisfy consumers' unanswered needs. Today, we shop, work, communicate, socialize, and entertain ourselves in dramatically different ways than we did in the industrial era—all because the nature and capabilities of the value creation system changed.

The point being, All-Star leaders stay in tune with those paradigm shifts because they rely on the MBA model to keep their leadership team, people, processes, and technology strategically aligned to the times.

Encompassing the virtues of the Du Pont industrial era financial system and the digital era system of the Balanced Scorecard, the MBA model adds a third dimension to the strategy process. The three dimensional lens of its strategy process—retrospective (Du Pont Financial), introspective (MBA quest), and prospective (Balanced Scorecard) enables leaders to see what other strategy models can't—pivotal views for pivotal times.

Like the 3D glasses in the 3D cinema university experiment, the MBA lens opens the mind of executive leaders to recognize not only unfulfilled customer needs, but also the alignment of the value creating assets (leadership, people, process, and technology) to service them. Recall in the Cross-Roads Allegory how difficult the All-Star consultant found it to convince a 2D minded Board to see his 3D viewpoint. A 2D mindset cannot appreciate the merits of a 3D vision, and its asset investment strategy and scorecard goals will both reflect that misalignment. The Balanced Scorecard does not check for bias and executive cataracts. But the MBA model does.

As we age, most of us need corrective lens to maintain clear sighted vision. So do leaders and their companies. Misaligned companies reflect the bias and closed mindedness that blind leaders over time. The three dimensional strategy process of the

MBA model removes those cataracts and restores the alignment of its customer focused assets.

It is not sufficient to understand MBA. If a company is to realize the full benefits of this powerful system, the leaders must embrace and believe in MBA. If the Leaders fully accept and submit themselves and the company to MBA, the company can attain and maintain sustainable competitive advantage over its competitors, because it will have a customer-centric, unique business model which, because it mirrors the beliefs, values, and personalities of the Leaders, cannot be duplicated.

Mission-Based Alignment frees Leaders to lead. The single most important responsibility of the CEO is to develop and promulgate the company's Mission. Communicating the Mission is a never-ending task. Every employee must understand and embrace the Mission with its values and priorities. Once this is understood throughout the company, then (and only then) employees can be empowered to make day-to-day decisions that will be in harmony with the Mission.

Mission-Based Alignment frees the leaders from day-to-day micro-management. It teaches the Managers that their primary function is to remove the obstacles that hinder the workers from performing efficiently and productively, and it shows the Managers how to do it. And by communicating the Mission, Strategy, and Values clearly and unambiguously to the workforce, Leaders and Managers empower the employees to fulfil the identified needs of the customer with high morale and a strong sense of worth and accomplishment, while reducing wasted efforts and wasted resources to a minimum.

Finally, MBA is the gift that keeps on giving. The longer that Leaders and Managers use MBA, the better they get at understanding the need of the customer and at honing the company's differentiation. The longer the customer experiences the rewards of doing business with the aligned company, the better they understand the company's Mission and their expectations become even more closely aligned with the company's performance. And the longer the employees hear the Leader talk to them about the customer need, the more they will understand the customer and the more they will trust that the Leaders and the Managers are walking their talk.

This is why the competitive advantage is sustainable. The aligned company keeps evolving and getting better and better. The competitor who tries to catch up by watching and emulating the aligned company can never catch up because they are attempting to emulate last year's model, while the aligned company has continued to grow and has become something else—an even better something else.

Aligned companies:

- Are mission-based;
- Know what they are and what they want to become;
- Keep focused;
- Place the customer first;
- Trust their employees;
- Communicate with their employees; and
- Empower their employees to serve the customer need.

Companies who do these things consistently rise to the top and stay there.